A King Production presents…

Stackin' Paper II
Genesis Payback

By

Joy Deja King

This novel is a work of fiction. Any references to real people, events, establishments, or locales are intended only to give the fiction a sense of reality and authenticity. Other names, characters, and incidents occurring in the work are either the product of the author's imagination or are used fictitiously, as those fictionalized events and incidents that involve real persons. Any character that happens to share the name of a person who is an acquaintance of the author, past or present, is purely coincidental and is in no way intended to be an actual account involving that person.

ISBN 10: 1-942217-98-6
ISBN 13: 978-1942217985
Cover concept by Joy Deja King & www.MarionDesigns.com
Cover model: Joy Deja King
Cover layout and graphic design by: www.MarionDesigns.com
Typesetting: Linda Williams
Editor: Dolly Lopez

Library of Congress Cataloging-in-Publication Data;
King, Joy Deja

Stackin' Paper: a novel by Joy Deja King
For complete Library of Congress Copyright info visit; www.joydejaking.com

A King Production
P.O. Box 912, Collierville, TN 38027

A King Production and the above portrayal log are trademarks of A King Production LLC

Copyright © 2022 by Joy Deja King. All rights reserved. No part of this book may be reproduced in any form without the permission from the publisher, except by reviewer who may quote brief passage to be printed in a newspaper or magazine.

Dedication

This Book is Dedicated To My:

Family, Readers and Supporters. I LOVE you guys so much. Please believe that!!

A KING PRODUCTION

Stackin' Paper II

Gen esis' Payback

Joy Deja King

Chapter One
Locked Up

"You need to get me the fuck up outta here! Not tomorrow, not next week, but motherfuckin' today!" CoCo barked into the phone.

"CoCo, you have to calm down. I'm on it. I have a few top-notch lawyers lined up, and I'm meeting with one of them tomorrow. Once I decide who I think is the best fit, I'll have them try and get you a bail."

"Chanel, what the fuck is taking so damn long? I've been locked up for a minute, and you still ain't secured me no representation. Shit, the type of paper we got access to—my bad—*you* got access to, because I don't have access to shit but a bunch of thirsty bitches being locked up in jail! The point is, I can afford the best lawyers money can buy, but yet you handling shit like a bitch is destitute."

"Chill! No I'm not. You know I got you. Right now you're being emotional, which is understandable, because the Feds got you caged up like an animal. But I promise I'm working on shit. I'm being smart, the way you taught me. I'm your sister, we're blood, and I guarantee you I will get you out of jail. Be patient."

"Okay. I trust you. You've never let me down. But I need you to make shit happen…soon."

"It will. I'ma come see you this weekend, so hold tight until then."

"Cool. And Chanel."

"Yes?"

"I love you."

"I love you too."

CoCo swallowed hard and stood with her head down for a moment after hanging up the phone. She slowly walked back to the 20x20 room that held twelve women, including her, which she dreaded. She couldn't believe the highlight of her day was waiting to get a 'cube', which was a partitioned area meant for one, now holding two, in a space of 8x6. But having even a tiny bit of privacy seemed like a small dose of sanity compared to what she was enduring now.

The confinement of a jail cell was in stark contrast

to the sprawling penthouse suite CoCo called home in an exclusive high-rise in Atlanta. Instead of residing on the top floor where there were only two other condos, she now had the top bunk, sharing her living quarters with over 450 women in a Federal Prison Camp built for 150. It was so bad, that they had taken all the recreation rooms and put beds inside of them. There was now talk that the TV rooms would also be made into cells. CoCo prayed that this place would be a distant memory by the time that new rule kicked in, but as each day passed her, optimism was turning into pessimism.

"Excuse me," CoCo said, to another inmate who was blocking her way from sitting down on the vinyl mat atop a solid metal flat.

"You're excused, if you let me hold a smoke."

CoCo was about to pop fire at the chick until she looked up and noticed the subtle smile on the lady's face. "Here you go," CoCo said, reaching in her pocket and handing the woman a cigarette.

"I'm glad you decided to make nice. I guess you've accepted the fact you're going to be here for a minute, and it's better to make friends than enemies."

"Nope, it was just a brief moment of kindness. Don't look too deep into it. Trust, I'm getting out this bitch. Me and jail cells don't mix. My people are working on it."

"I wouldn't count on that. There are women that have been locked up in here for years, and don't nobody come see them. I mean, they haven't seen their kids since they hit them front doors. It's like they forgot who the fuck you are. It's crazy. We got the men's prison right next door, and they stay packed with visitors. But don't nobody wanna come see us. Even in prison, females get the short end of the stick."

CoCo eyed the Hispanic woman who didn't look any more than thirty. She might've been younger, but her, hardened features and the extra pounds of weight carried aged you. She was tempted to ask the woman how she ended up in this fucked up predicament, but decided against it. The last thing she wanted was for her to get the wrong idea and think they were going to be jailhouse buddies.

"I hear you, but that's not my situation. My sister, Chanel is holding me down, and she *will* get me out of here as soon as possible, that I can promise you. So no, I ain't interested in making friends, because I'm only passing through."

"I've heard many women kick that same line, and five years later they still calling this place home, or have been transferred to another dungeon just like this one. But hey, maybe your situation is different. I wish you the best of luck, but until then, you locked up like the rest of us."

CoCo laid back on the flimsy mattress that

was supposed to be a bed. There was a burning sensation in the pit of her stomach at the idea of trading in her previous life to live in this hellhole for eternity. She had no choice but to believe Chanel would save her from this misery, or else she would surely start hearing death knocking at the door.

*****

Genesis took a long pull from his Newport. It was his third one in less than an hour. All he seemed to be able to do for the last few weeks was smoke and think. Being holed up in a motel room with no access to the real world was taking a toll on him. But he was a wanted man, and his options were limited

"What the fuck! This cheap ass television don't never fuckin' work!" he screamed, tossing the remote control across the room. He slumped down on the bed, frustrated and beat. Watching television was his only real connection to human life, but that shit was inconsistent. Sometimes the TV would come the fuck on, and sometimes that shit stayed the fuck off. It was unreliable, like everything else in his life.

As the walls began squeezing in on him, Genesis

was rattled out of his discouraging thoughts by the vibration of his cell phone. It was a sound he welcomed, since he had been waiting patiently for the call.

"Yo, what's good?" Genesis said composed, with no indication in his voice that overwhelming stress was consuming him.

"Everything has been arranged. We can move forward tomorrow."

"That's what I needed to hear. You know where to find me. I'll be ready." Genesis ended the call, and for the first time in months, he was able to exhale without a stiffened ache in his chest taking effect. He knew shit was far from sweet, but besides a grave or a jail cell, anything was an upgrade from the gutter he was stashed at now.

Chapter Two
Boss Lady

Tonya sat back in the leather massage chair with her eyes closed as the Chinese woman placed the steaming hot towel over her lower leg. She was long overdue for a pedicure, and relished every moment of feeling somewhat alive again.

Since Deuce had been killed, Tonya had no interest in pampering herself, even in the simplest forms. For the last few months, she had completely shut herself off from friends and family, only finding solace in the constant flashes of the intimate moments she shared with him. The cramp in her heart was even worsened by the fact that no one had been arrested and held responsible for the murder of the man she planned on spending the rest of her life with.

Tonya looked down at the engagement ring still adorning her finger. She didn't have the strength to take it off. She clearly remembered each word Deuce had spoken, the exact clothes he was wearing, and the genuine love in his eyes when he got down on bended knee and asked her to marry him. Never did she believe that day would come, but it did. Deuce had wanted her to be his wife, but that would never be, because somebody snatched her dreams away in a split second. The only thing that kept her going was the determination to bring down the person or people responsible for taking away the man she loved more than anything in this world.

"Girl, that nigga fuck wit' too many bitches."

"Yeah, you right, but at least he believes in coughing up them coins."

The familiar voices and the sounds of the bells chiming from the door opening and closing made Tonya open her eyes and look up. Her intense stare filled the nail salon and caused the women to stop their conversation to see what direction the uneasy energy was coming from.

Monica was the first one to zoom in on Tonya's face, and when Denise caught a hint of it, her first response was to turn around and walk the fuck out. The three women hadn't seen each other since

Deuce's funeral, and no one seemed interested in a reunion.

"Hey, Tonya, it's good to see you," Monica said flatly, trying to chip away at the awkward moment.

At first Tonya remained mute, and Denise reached for Monica's arm, indicating to her that it was time to go.

"Hey, long time no see," Tonya finally responded.

But Denise didn't care. She had no desire to share her space with Tonya.

"Do you ladies want manicure and pedicure?" the Chinese lady asked, catching the women off guard.

"Actually, we can't..."

"Just a pedicure," Monica answered, cutting Denise off before she could finish her sentence.

"What are you doing?" Denise mumbled in a low tone.

"We're here now, and I can't have my feet looking fucked up at this party we're going to tonight. Now relax," Monica whispered, trying not to make it so obvious that neither one of them wanted to be there.

The Chinese lady pointed to the empty seats, which would have Tonya positioned in the middle, and Monica and Denise on either side of her.

"So, how have you been, Tonya?" asked Monica, as she tried to portray a level of easiness.

"Hanging in there, but a moment doesn't go by that I don't think about Deuce."

"I feel you. I still can't believe he's gone." Monica glanced down and caught a glimpse of the sparkler on Tonya's finger. "I see you're still wearing his ring."

"Yeah. You know he got murdered on the same day we got engaged."

Monica nodded her head, feeling all sorts of uncomfortable, and hoping this very subject would be avoided.

"Not to be rude, but seriously Tonya, don't you think it's time to take the ring off?" Denise's pleasant tone didn't lessen the cutting effect her words had.

"Excuse me, what did you say?" Tonya turned to her left, wanting to look Denise directly in her face.

"Girl, she didn't say nothing," Monica interjected, wanting to snatch Denise up for even going there.

But Denise wouldn't let up. "Tonya, I understand you're going through a hard time, and letting go can't be easy, but Deuce isn't coming back. And wearing the engagement ring he gave you ain't gon' change that," she stated brightly, as if she was telling Tonya to do something as simple as pass her some nail polish.

"I see your simple ass ain't changed a bit!" Tonya spit back.

"Oh Lord, here we go!" Monica mumbled,

dreading the fireworks that were bound to start going off.

"Was that comment really necessary? I'm keeping it a hundred percent wit' you and stating the obvious, but you want to take stabs at me. Dude has been buried for a few months now, and he was your brand new fiancé, not long-term husband. You wasn't even his baby mama! Get the fuck over it! I mean, you still rockin' a dead man's ring. That's a tad bit delusional."

"I know you ain't throwing around words like 'delusional'. You the same trick that was running around stalking Genesis after he tossed you out like the trash you are. Then you stepped to his official girl, Talisa, who had not only stepped in your shoes, but wore them quite nicely. Oh, my fault! She didn't have to step in your shoes, because you didn't own them to begin with. You were only some side piece pussy, never the main entrée."

"And you was only the babysitter, never the baby maker, if my memory serves me correctly. No wonder he put a ring on your finger. It would be cheaper to marry you than to pay for fulltime child care."

The Chinese lady polishing Tonya's toes almost messed up her meticulous French pedicure from getting so caught up in the catty exchange between the two women.

"Both of you need to fall back. You taking this way too far." Monica was trying to be the voice of reason, but neither woman cared.

"Monica, I don't have no beef with you, besides the fact that for whatever reason, you continue to hang around this loser. But she is completely out-of-line. It ain't none of her business why I still want to wear the ring Deuce gave me."

"And it ain't none of your business what went down between me and Genesis. You always like to throw that shit up in my face and I'm sick of it!"

"I was talking to Monica. If you would have kept your mouth shut, then I wouldn't have brought Genesis' name up."

"Enough of this back and forth. The two of you don't like each other…fine. Just don't say anything to one another so this bickering will end," Monica huffed, lying back in her seat.

Tonya and Denise slit their eyes at one another before sitting back in their chairs. All three women would have been better off going their separate ways, but the damage done in the past seemed to keep their lives intertwined in the present.

*****

Chanel sat in the prestigious law firm, waiting

to meet with the attorney Arnez had referred her to. She eyed her diamond face watch, growing impatient, although she was the one that had been forty-five minutes late. She was contemplating whether to get up and walk out, when the receptionist made eye contact with her.

"Mr. Katz can see you now. He'll be out shortly."

"Which one is it? Is he ready for me now, or is he coming, 'cause it can't be both?"

The demure blonde was thrown off by Chanel's brazen question. She had repeated that same line to over a dozen clients, and they would all give her a gracious smile and continue to wait, so she was dumbstruck at how to reply. "Umm, well, he's wrapping things up with a client, and he'll be right out."

"Oh, so you meant to say he'll be ready for me soon, not right now." Chanel sighed. She had no problem making others wait, but hadn't learned how to return the favor.

A few minutes later when the attorney walked out, the receptionist immediately perked up, as she felt extremely intimidated being alone in Chanel's presence.

"Ms. Armstrong, it's a pleasure to meet you. Follow me, please," Mr. Katz said, extending his hand.

When Chanel stood up, she towered over the miniature sized attorney. Part of it was due to his lack of height, but it didn't help his cause that Chanel had on her Roma five-inch high open-toe Gucci sandals with bamboo detail. Her thick, sturdy, sculpted legs made her steps seem effortless, even in the stiletto heels.

When they entered the office, Mr. Katz sat down behind his rectangular glass desk, which actually made him appear much taller and very powerful. Chanel took a seat and placed her large wrap framed sunglasses down, crossing her legs, making her mid-length black skirt rise up. Mr. Katz couldn't help but look down, staring approvingly at the ebony beauty.

"What can I do for you, Ms. Armstrong?"

"Make sure that my sister stays locked up."

"Excuse me?"

"You heard me correctly."

"This is a first. Most people come to me in hopes they can keep somebody *out* of jail, not keep them *in*."

"I'm not most people."

"When I spoke to Arnez, I was under the impression that you wanted to retain my services for your sister, CoCo."

"That's true."

"Then when your sister becomes my client, I have to do what is in her best interest. If that means I can get her out of jail, then that's what I'm going to do. And quite frankly, after reviewing some of the information I was able to get a hold of, the case against your sister is looking rather thin. Especially since the star witness, an umm…" Mr. Katz opened up a manila folder on his desk, flipping through some papers before looking back up, "Antwon Walker is now deceased."

"Listen, Mr. Katz, I have no problem with you getting my sister out of jail…eventually. But right now, it's not safe for her to be in the streets. I simply want you to stall some so I can make preparations for her release."

Mr. Katz gave Chanel a puzzling gaze, as if he wasn't sold on the idea.

"Arnez is one of your top clients, and I'm sure you know he's a very close friend of mine."

"Your point?"

"The same way Arnez would want you to take care of my needs, he would also want me to take care of yours."

Mr. Katz let his eyes wander back down to the curves on the tempting, deep brown thighs. Salacious thoughts instantly began swarming through his mind, and Chanel was well aware of that. But not wanting him to get too excited and bust a nutt in his thirty-five hundred-dollar custom made suit, she opened up the snap on her sand python purse. The tassels with bamboo details and metal plates swayed as she dropped it on top of the desk as she pulled out the check she had already written and signed.

"I think this will be more than enough for you to feel fully compensated for your time and services." Chanel handed the check to Mr. Katz, and there was no doubt that all the zeros did bring a smile to his face, but he couldn't help but think getting between Chanel's legs would bring even a bigger smile.

"Yes indeed, I will begin building a defense for your sister and start discovery on the prosecution's case. I'll also set up a visit with your sister so she'll know she's in good hands."

"Excellent! But just remember, you work for *me*." Those were Chanel's parting words as she made her exit from Mr. Katz's office.

Chapter Three
Where Did He Go

When the car arrived at three o'clock in the morning to pick up Genesis, he was anxious to leave, and at the same time, apprehensive about where he would be going. But his choices were limited. There weren't too many people he trusted to make sure he could relocate to a safe place while he figured shit out.

From the stress of being on the run and missing the woman he loved more than anything in this world, he still hadn't had time to properly grieve over losing his best friend. Genesis wanted to personally have the blood on his hands of the person responsible for killing Deuce, and being caged up didn't allow that possibility.

For the past few months, Genesis replayed in his head every word that was exchanged between him and Deuce at the Buffalo Billiards that night. That was the happiest he had seen him in so long. He was finally ready to settle down, and shared the news about asking Tonya to marry him. He was engaged, his money was right, and life was good. So good, that they both got caught slipping and didn't see the warning signs that Antwon had turned into a snitch. Genesis doubted that cost Deuce his life, but it definitely was making it impossible for him to move forward with his.

Not only had Antwon sold them out on the drug front, he also informed the Feds about all the stash houses and warehouse where he kept his bread — millions of dollars all confiscated and gone. The only money Genesis had was what he took from his condo when he bolted before the Feds ran up in there.

It hurt him to his heart to leave Talisa in the middle of the night and disappear, leaving her to wonder where he went and if he would ever come back. Genesis had planned to come back for Talisa a long time ago, but when he realized he had no money, shit changed dramatically. He needed a legal eagle that could soar him through the fucked up predicament he was in, and that would take serious paper, not the hundred-thousand-dollars he had escaped with. Trying to keep his head above water had that money quickly dwindling away.

Now here he was, on his way to the airport to catch a redeye. He hated having to go so far away from Talisa, because even though she didn't know it, twice a week he would sit in a parked car across the street and watch her come in and out of the building. So many times he wanted to run out of the car and just hold her and feel the touch of her lips against his, but he knew the Feds were watching. Genesis was in full disguise, so although they didn't notice him, he definitely recognized them.

As Genesis walked over to the counter inside the airport, he rationalized that this would only be a brief separation until he could get shit back on track. Because once he did make it back to Talisa, it would be without fear that he would be hauled off in handcuffs, serving a bid for the rest of his life.

"Sir, may I see your ticket and ID please?" the lady asked as Genesis calmly handed over the requested material. His throat was dry, and although he was confident that his connect had come through, there was always the possibility that shit could and would go terribly wrong.

"Will you be checking any bags, Mr. Williams?"

"No, just a carry-on."

"Well then, here's your boarding pass, and enjoy

your flight."

The woman's courteous smile as she handed Genesis back his ID and boarding pass made his insides mellow out just a tad. He was ready to catch his flight, and felt he was finally about to put himself in a position to fight for his freedom.

Chapter Four
When Opportunity Knocks

"The baby is fine, but I'm concerned. Your weight gain is extremely low, especially to be in your second trimester," the doctor explained to Talisa.

Talisa looked down at her frail body. Her stomach only had a slight bulge that you wouldn't even notice unless you saw her naked. "As long as the baby is healthy, that's all that matters."

"No, the baby needs for you to be healthy too. I'm not trying to intrude in your personal life, but I am your doctor, and I can't help but be somewhat worried. Most women by this point in their pregnancy are gaining weight. You're losing it. Is it stressed related?"

Talisa stared at her doctor for a few seconds.

There was no doubt in her mind that the middle-aged black woman was genuinely concerned about the wellbeing of her and her unborn child. But am I suppose to say, *I'm stressed the fuck out due to the fact that my baby daddy is on the run from the Feds because he's a drug kingpin?* Talisa wasn't ready to share that information with anybody yet, including her doctor. Not even her parents knew she was pregnant. She was carrying the burden alone.

"I'll start taking better care of myself, Dr. Johnson. I just stopped having morning sickness and I haven't had an appetite. But the nausea is settling down, so I'm sure by my next visit, I will have gained some weight." Talisa wasn't sure if the doctor believed her story, but it was partially true. She hadn't had an appetite since Genesis left her, and in all honesty, some days she didn't even want to live. But knowing his baby was growing inside of her made her try, but she had to try harder if she wanted to deliver a healthy baby.

"I hope so, Talisa, for your sake and the sake of your child. And if you ever need someone to talk to, I'm a pretty good listener."

"Thank you, I'll keep that in mind."

*****

"Can you believe that ho ass heffa! She tryna put me on blast about Genesis, and her crazy ass still wearing an engagement ring from a dead as dirt nigga. Get the fuck outta here! I can't stand Tonya's ass!" Denise yelled, staring at her reflection in the mirror as she applied makeup to her face.

"You know how Tonya felt about Deuce. You shouldn't have said shit to her."

"Motherfucker, you the one who commented on her ring first," Denise reminded Monica.

"True, but I didn't say it in no derogatory way. I was just a little shocked to see that she was still rockin' his ring, so it slipped out."

"Whatever!"

"But yo, you need to be careful about what you say around her. If Tonya ever found out that you played a role in her man getting killed, you know she's going postal."

"That's why I wanted to turn the fuck around when we saw her at the nail salon. But yo' ass wanted to stay."

"Because we've been avoiding her since the funeral. I don't want her to start getting suspicious."

"I feel you. But honestly, Deuce's murder was not my fault. I had no idea that Arnez was going to try and kill Genesis, let alone fuck around and take him and Antwon out in the process."

"Well, fuck Antwon! I heard from a few niggas that he was a snitch anyway, and that's why

Genesis on the run now. But won't none of that matter to Tonya. She ain't gonna care that you thought you was doing some harmless plotting on Genesis. All she gonna know is that her man is dead, and you conspired with the nigga that made it happen."

Denise knew Monica was right, and although she wouldn't admit it, the guilt ate her up damn near everyday. Her jealousy, bitterness and immaturity played right into Arnez's hands, and he used it to the fullest.

"Girl, all this talk about Tonya and dead folks is ruining my high," Denise said taking a pull off her blunt. "We have a party to attend, and rehashing shit we can't do nothing about ain't got no place here." Denise hoped that if they could stop talking about the past, she could pretend it no longer existed, But everybody knows the past is always waiting to catch up to the future.

When Denise and Monica pulled up to the lounge in downtown Philly, Denise immediately started scoping out what the vehicle game was looking like. "I only see a couple of hot whips," she commented.

"Tech said most of his dudes were coming through, and he's stackin' paper, so I'm assuming they are too," Monica shrugged.

"Girl, we in a recession. Don't nobody got time for assuming. You see this face?" Denise pointed as she turned towards Monica, who was in the driver's seat. "I didn't beat this shit to death for an assumption. I need results!"

"I did my part. We're here. Shit, at first Tech didn't even want me coming. I know it's because he's gonna have a handful of his other chicks up in this spot, but whatever!"

"At least you got somebody. You know they cut my hours down at the store, and who knows if or when they gonna increase them. Shit is so tight for me right now…"

"I know! I'm the one who's been carrying your part of the rent for the last two months. Shit, I'm 'Team Denise'! Don't nobody want you to find a qualified sponsor more than me."

"Well, I damn sure ain't gonna find him sitting in this car with you, so let's go."

Denise and Monica strolled through the dimly lit lounge on two different missions. Monica was looking for her semi-man, Tech, and Denise was looking to find a man. Neither seemed to be making any progress until Monica noticed a familiar looking hand rubbing up on an ample ass. What made the hand so familiar was the blinding diamond watch on his wrist. Even from the distance between them, the custom-made blue diamond ice slapped her in the face.

"I'll be back," Monica smacked, quickly walking off.

"Where you going?" But Monica was halfway to her destination before Denise had completed her question. She watched the direction Monica was going as she slid over by the bar. She felt awkward standing in the middle of the floor alone. Even though she wanted to show off her teal, low-cut mini-dress in an attempt to lure a man in, but she had played the game long enough to know that looking lonely and desperate wasn't the way to do it.

"Can I get a Malibu with pineapple juice?" Denise told the bartender. She figured that a drink in her hand and sexily grinding to the music would make her appear as if she was enjoying herself. And one thing she knew was that most men, especially ballers, loved to fuck with a girl that knew how to have a good time. With her petite but voluptuous assets slithering to the beat, Denise soon noticed that more eyes were swaying in her direction. But her situation called for alerting the right eyes.

Soon, a few dudes started stepping to her, offering to buy a drink or initiating small talk, but she knew money from broke motherfuckers, and the cats stepping her way were what she labeled 'the barely getting by'. They were using every little dollar they earned — rather it was from being a low-level drug dealer or working a blue collar job—to pretend like they were making money, when in all actuality, they were barely getting by.

Denise was quickly becoming distressed that nothing was popping off for her. She hadn't come across one option, not even a potential option. She was ready to tell Monica to come on, but she could see that she was having a heated confrontation with Tech. Still not wanting to look stupid, she decided to order another drink that she couldn't really afford. She literally had every dime to her name in her pocket, and it needed to last until payday.

"I'll have another," Denise said, throwing caution to the wind.

"I'll get that for you." Denise didn't even bother to turn around when she heard the male voice, figuring it was another buster wasting her time, but then from the corner of her eye, she caught a glimpse of his Prada loafers, and optimism started to kick in.

"That's okay, I can buy my own drink," she hissed, nonchalantly. Denise knew she was taking a chance trying to play the hard-to-get role, but if her gut instincts were on point, she was gambling for big money instead of small fries.

"I didn't say that you couldn't, I was only offering."

"Thanks for the offer, but I decline." Denise still wasn't giving the dude any real face time. She was giving him half-face glances while waiting for the bartender to give her the drink.

"I can dig that. So, you're declining my drink offer, but can you give me a name?"

"Listen," Denise popped with an attitude as she finally turned around full frontal. "I'm not interested in a drink, and I'm not interested in giving you my name. As a matter-of-fact, could you carry on?"

The dude stood looking perplexed as hell. And Denise knew exactly why. The nigga was straight-up fine. When she first turned around, she wanted to drop her panties and ride his dick right there in the club, but a little voice in her head kept saying to stick to the plan, so that's what she did.

"Oh, you must be here wit' yo' man," he stated as if there could be no other reason a woman would turn him down.

"No, I'm here with my homegirl. No offense, but I'm not in the mood to entertain no hard-up regular dude."

"Offense taken. Words like 'hard-up' and 'regular' should never be used to describe me."

There was no need to convince Denise of that. He didn't know it, but she had already sized him up with every detail included. She knew he was something proper, and rejection wasn't even an alternative for him. That's why she counted on her approach working the magic that she needed.

"I apologize. I didn't mean to offend you, but I really need to be going. My friend is waiting for me." Denise began walking away, when she felt a gentle but firm grip on her arm.

"Wait, we're not finished here."

"Yes, we are, unless you can give me a reason to stay."

"If you would slow your roll and give me a chance, I can give you thousands and thousands of reasons to stay."

"You sound pretty confident."

"I only spit facts, and that makes me very confident."

"Well now, you have my full attention. You have to either put up or shut up. What's it gonna be?"

"Are you leaving with me?" That request seemed so simple, but the blaze in his eyes made it so intense.

"I don't even know your name."

"I don't know yours either, but if you come with me, you'll find out."

"I'm right by your side," Denise said, placing her glass down on the nearby table. She glanced behind her shoulder, and Monica was still riding Tech's ass. "Wait, hold up. I need to tell my friend that I'm leaving."

"Where's she at?"

"Over there with that dude."

"Who, Tech?"

"Yeah. You cool with him?"

"No doubt! That's my man! We handle a lot of business together. Don't worry about your friend, she's in good hands."

Denise nodded her head in agreement. *I got deals to close. I'll text her later,* she thought to herself, and headed out the door with whom Denise hoped would turn out to be her savior.

Chapter Five
Return The Favor

Genesis woke up from getting some of the best sleep he had had since being on the run. Resting his head on a firm king sized mattress with fifteen-hundred thread count sheets will do that for you.

"This damn sure ain't the outskirts of Philly," Genesis said, pulling back the curtains on the huge window overlooking the beach. His connect went beyond and delivered on his promise to provide him with comfortable accommodations. The spacious house on the beach gave him the tranquility his mind needed to put the pieces to the puzzle together.

When Genesis arrived at LAX, he had no idea

where the tinted black SUV was taking him. But he soon realized they were headed to Malibu. It was indeed the perfect hideaway. No one would expect that was where he was resting his head, and that was the plan.

Genesis eyed the clock and decided to get in the shower because his connect would be coming over to meet with him shortly. He couldn't decide what he found more appealing; being back in the sort of beautiful surroundings he had grown accustomed to from living the life of a rich hustler, or finally having a face-to-face conversation with another human being that wasn't a stranger.

Genesis stayed in the shower longer than he had planned, but he was appreciating the great water pressure he had been deprived of for so long from being in rundown motels. When he stepped out of the shower and stared in the mirror, he was pleased that his body was holding up. He hadn't been able to keep up his workout regimen by going to the gym, so he did old fashion pushups and sit-ups to maintain his sculpted six-two physique.

"Damn, all this shit is nice, and in my size," Genesis commented when he opened up the closet door and inspected the clothes that had already been purchased for him. The items still had the tags on them. He decided to put on a pair of taupe linen draw-string pants and a crisp white T-shirt. He looked comfortable yet sexy in the attire.

Right as he was finishing up, he heard the doorbell ring. He headed downstairs and although he knew who it was, out of habit he had to double check before opening the door.

"No need to worry, it's only me," the man said, when Genesis opened the door.

"Why didn't you just come in? I know you have a key."

"This is your place for now, and you deserve your privacy, so I won't be using my key as long as you're staying here. Unless, of course, an emergency comes up," he stated, stepping inside the foyer.

"I appreciate that, Quentin. I also appreciate you helping me out like this. Never did I think it would be you who would step up and handle shit for me."

"Ever since CoCo hooked us up, we've done a lot of business together. You've always conducted your business straight-up. And trust me, not too many men are doing that, especially these days. The difference between my generation of so called gangsters and this new generation is in stark contrast. But you," he pointed his index finger in Genesis' direction, "Could step back to my time when I was your age, and dominate the streets with me. Your business character is just that strong. When CoCo said I would mesh with you, she was a hundred percent right, and I can't say that about many people."

"I got the legendary Quentin Jacobs giving me compliments like that! Shit, can't nobody tell me nothing!" Genesis smiled.

"I only speak the truth. But on to more important things, like getting you the legal counsel you need. I've retained a lawyer for you. He's already begun working on your case. I'll probably bring him over to meet with you later on this week."

"I'm not ready to turn myself into the Feds."

"And you won't have to. If I have my way, you won't spend one day behind bars. Trust me; if anybody can get you off, it's this attorney. His grandfather is a retired Federal Judge, and his father is still on the bench. His connections run long and deep."

"Wow! Retaining him must've cost you a fortune. I feel like shit that I don't have any money to contribute," Genesis snarled, standing up from the couch and shaking his head.

"Don't worry about that. You can always make more money, but freedom is priceless."

"Speaking of freedom, any word on what's going on with CoCo?"

"I reached out to Chanel to offer whatever support she might need, but she assured me that she was handling the situation and had everything under control."

"Glad to hear that. But CoCo is in good hands.

From the first day I met them, Chanel always had her sister's back. She's gonna make sure CoCo gets out of jail, even if she gotta bust her out herself."

"You got that right. Chanel is a beast when it comes to protecting CoCo," Quentin laughed quietly. "But listen, there was something else I wanted to talk to you about."

"Sounds serious. What is it?"

"I need you to do me a favor."

"Of course. But I don't know how helpful I can be under my current circumstances."

"I can set everything up. I just need for you to do it."

"Anything. I'm a free man living in luxury because of you. All you have to do is say the word, and I'm on it."

"That's what I wanted to hear. I want you to take a look at this picture," Quentin said, opening his briefcase.

Genesis walked over to where Quentin was sitting, and watched him take out a 4x6 photo of a young lady.

"I need you to locate her."

"No disrespect, Quentin, but wouldn't you be better off hiring a private investigator?"

"I tried that, and they had no luck. It's like she disappeared off the face of the earth."

"What makes you think I would have better luck?"

"Because the last person she was living with is a heavy hitter in the music industry. They were staying in Beverly Hills, but they've both vanished. I have a lot of connects, but nobody in the entertainment business. But I had some of my people do some asking around…"

"And you heard that I have somewhat of a close relationship with T-Roc," Genesis said, finishing his sentence.

"Exactly. I'll take you to him, and maybe he can shed some light on where the man is, because there is no doubt in my mind this young lady won't be far behind."

"If you don't want to answer, just say so and I'll back off. But who is she, and why do you need to find her?"

"Her name is Maya, and she's my daughter. I recently found out that her brother is dead, and he was the only family she really had. I want to make sure she's okay."

"From that statement, I take it that the two of you don't have a close relationship."

"We have no relationship at all. She has no idea I'm her father…it's a long story. But when her brother was alive, I was always able to keep tabs on her. Now that's he's dead, I don't know anything. But the last time I saw him, he told me she was living with a man named Supreme in Beverly Hills."

"Supreme, the rapper turned music mogul?"

"I'm assuming that's who it is."

"Is your daughter married to him?"

"No, unless it happened recently, because Mike would have told me if she had gotten married."

"I could've sworn Supreme was married. About a year or so ago, it was all on the news that his daughter had been kidnapped. I saw him and his wife on television together asking the public for help in locating her. That was a big story."

"If he is married, that wouldn't be hard to find out. But my only concern right now is locating my daughter and making sure she's okay. Will you help me?"

"That's not even a question you need to ask me. I *will* find your daughter. I can guarantee you that."

Chapter Six
No Need In The Facts

Arnez sat quietly at a corner table eating his lunch. Dining at Lacroix at the Rittenhouse had become almost a daily ritual whenever he was in town. He loved the international cuisine, combining Spanish, Portuguese, Thai and American flavors to create a truly distinctive mouthwatering feast. And the ambiance was his style, which was elegant yet laid back in the prestigious Rittenhouse hotel looking out over the downtown square. Normally he would eat alone, with only his bodyguard accompanying him, but today he had his faithful ride or die chick by his side.

"Chanel, are you sure you don't want to eat anything?"

"Positive. You know I like simple food, nothing too fancy. But I will have some more wine."

"You don't think it's too early to be drinking?"

"Anytime after noon is open season, and it's already two o'clock."

"As long as you're alert, we're good."

"I'm always alert. You don't *ever* have to worry about that."

Arnez gave a slight smile, knowing that Chanel wasn't exaggerating. He would never trust anybody completely with his life, but if he had a top three list, she would easily come in at number one. She had proven her loyalty to him on more than one occasion. The ultimate substantiation came for Arnez when she turned on her own sister so that he could have what he wanted—to take over her drug business.

"You never told me how your meeting with Robert went."

"Who?" she asked, not recognizing the name.

"Robert Katz."

"Oh, the attorney. It went decent. At first he didn't seem to be on the same page as me, but once I put the check in his hand, he seemed to wise up."

"Yeah, money has a way of doing that to people. So, what did he think of CoCo's case?"

"He seemed to think the prosecution's case is weak. You know, with Antwon being dead and all."

"I guess you can blame me for that one. I still can't believe my people fucked around and took out the wrong man," Arnez said in a low tone. Even though no one was around to hear their conversation, he remained cautious. "So, instead of that nigga, Genesis being dead, he's on the run, and with the right attorney, he'll probably beat the case."

"It takes money to do that, and from what I heard, the Feds ran up in every spot he had and took all his money. That means the nigga's broke, and broke defendants don't win federal court cases."

"True indeed. But I hope he resurfaces before the Feds get hold of him, because I'd much rather see him dead than locked up in jail."

Chanel couldn't help but roll her eyes on the sly. She knew that the only reason Arnez wanted Genesis dead was because he felt that he stole his woman. His infatuation with Talisa kept him determined to see Genesis six feet under.

"I think we have more important problems to worry about than how Genesis meets his demise," she said.

"You're right, and one of our problems just walked in," Arnez said, nodding his head towards the front entry.

Chanel discreetly turned to see who he was

talking about without being obvious. She recognized the man who was accompanied by a young woman. "Ain't that some shit! Your biggest rival likes to eat at the same restaurant as you."

"Stay right here. I'ma go speak." Arnez got up from his chair, and his bodyguard was two steps behind, making sure his boss was protected at all times. "Delondo, how are you?" Arnez gave a pleasant smile, as if speaking to a friend instead of an enemy.

"I'm good. I see you have good taste in food."

"Of course! This place is one of the best, if not *the* best. Well, I won't keep you. I saw you come in and just wanted to say hello."

"Thanks. Oh, how rude of me. Denise, this is Arnez. Arnez, this is Denise. Baby, we're in the same line of business together."

Arnez reached out and shook Denise's hand, giving no indication that they already knew each other, to Denise's relief. "Nice meeting you," she grinned, trying not to appear nervous. The last thing Denise wanted to do was fuck up her new found fortune with Delondo.

When she first met him a few weeks ago in the club, Denise had a feeling he was doing big things, but never on the level she soon discovered he was ballin' on. She had been playing him so smoothly that she had suckered Delondo to start believing she was wifey material. And luckily for her, Monica had never put her business out there to Tech, so she didn't have anybody contradicting the image she was portraying. Denise knew that if it was revealed she had any prior dealings with Arnez, Delondo would start asking a million questions, and he wouldn't like any of the answers she would have to give.

"Nice to meet you too. I won't hold you all up any longer. It was good seeing you, Delondo."

"Good seeing you too." Both men gave each other a counterfeit smile, knowing they would love it if the other one met their fate of death tomorrow. "Fake ass nigga...I need to smoke his ass!" Delondo mumbled after Arnez was out of earshot.

"I take it you don't like him."

"Hell fuckin' no! That nigga been on my shit ever since I came down here and started regulating these streets. He needs to take his country ass back to Atlanta before I send him back in a body bag!" Delondo stated in a thick New York accent.

Oh, hell no! This nigga can't ever find out that I had any sort of dealings with Arnez. My phony good girl persona has been working, and I don't need for my spot to be blown up at this point. Shiiit, I haven't even fucked the nigga yet, even though I'm dying too. But holding out on the pussy has got this nigga wining and dining me. If I knew that keeping the legs locked would get me these sorts of results, I would've been practicing this shit a long time ago, thought Denise as she watched Arnez sit down at his table, praying she would never see his face again.

"How did it go over there?" Chanel inquired when Arnez sat down.

"Rather interesting."

"Why is that?"

"Because that woman he's with is who helped me set up Genesis."

"Really now! That is interesting. Did you let Delondo know that she knew you?"

"Fuck no! She was probably about to piss on herself wondering if I was going to let her new man know she sold out her old one for all of twenty-five hundred dollars. Clearly, by bringing her here he doesn't know he's dealing with a low rent ho."

"So, are you going to tell him? I would think you would get a kick out of letting Delondo know he's running around sportin' a disloyal, cheap trick."

"His stupidity is going to be my gain. Maybe last time I wasn't able to close the deal on Genesis using Denise's information, but I won't make the same mistake with Delondo."

"I highly doubt she's going to sell out Delondo. Besides Genesis, I'm sure he's the biggest catch she's ever had. She's not fucking that up."

"She's not going to have a choice. Because if Denise doesn't help me, she'll lose him anyway once I let Delondo know that load he's carrying isn't a treasure, but trash. So, Denise will give us the prize. But while I work on that, we need to begin making our move to immobilize Delondo now."

"I couldn't agree with you more."

*****

CoCo lay on her bunk, flipping through some random tabloid magazine that one of the inmates had left laying around. She didn't recognize half of the faces or names, because following pop-culture wasn't her thing. But she had read every magazine she had in her pile a zillion times, and needed something new.

"Armstrong, your attorney is here," the guard announced, causing CoCo to rise up in shock. She tossed the magazine down and waited for a few seconds before standing up, making sure she heard the guard correctly. "Armstrong, your attorney is here!" the guard yelled, this time to make sure CoCo heard her.

CoCo stood up and followed the guard to a private room that she had witnessed a couple of other inmates go into, but in the months she had been there, she had never seen the insides of it, until now. She sized up the diminutive attorney, but by the design of his suit, she knew that there was nothing small about his pockets.

"Ms. Armstrong, I'm Mr. Katz, your attorney." He greeted her with confidence, which CoCo at once took a liking to. He gave her a firm handshake, and CoCo took a seat.

"I'm relieved to finally have some representation up in here. I was beginning to think my sister didn't want me to get the fuck out."

Mr. Katz couldn't tell if CoCo was being serious with her statement, since whether she knew it or not, there was some validity to it. "No, that's not the case. Your sister retained my services because she does want you to come home a free woman, and if anyone can make that happen, it's me."

"So, how is my case looking?" CoCo wanted to get down to the facts. Hearing his personal endorsement of what he could make happen wasn't going to get her out of prison. What he would make happen was.

"I've begun discovery on the prosecution's case, and everything is pretty much centered on what was told to them by Antwon Walker. I'm sure you're aware that Mr. Walker is now deceased, so that weakens their case a great deal. Yes, they have the statements he made, but a defendant has the right to confront their accuser, and with him being dead, we've been denied that right."

"So what? Can you get the case dismissed?"

"I don't see it being that easy. The prosecution isn't going to want to dismiss this case. They're accusing you and your co-defendant, Genesis Taylor of running a multi-million dollar drug enterprise. They're charging him with kingpin status, and you with queen-pin. Having dealt with cases similar to this in the past, I believe the prosecutor's next move is to try to get Mr. Taylor to cop a plea and turn on you."

"Is he in custody?"

"No, in fact he's on the run. But trust me, he will get caught, because there are only so many places a wanted man can hide. But that's why I believe they will try to make a deal with him first because of the additional charges he'll be facing."

"Well, if they're building their case against me thinking Genesis will flip, then they fucked up in the game. Genesis is a warrior. He would never turn against me," CoCo said, without a hint of doubt in her voice.

"I've seen these federal prosecutors turn brother against brother in courtrooms. When they start using terms like 'twenty-five years to life behind bars, away from your family and loved ones', the strongest men become putty in the prosecutor's hands."

"I know all about weak people. In my business,

not to know is a costly liability. Trust me, if the Feds are counting on Genesis to be their saving grace, they're in for a rude awakening."

"I hope you're right, because without his cooperation, it's going to be tough to get the charges against you to stick. But if he doesn't talk, then they'll come to you next with an offer."

"And you already know my answer is, hell no! I ain't no snitch. I loathe a snitch, you feel me? Now, what's up with bail? Since you claim to be so good, I know you can get me that."

"I do believe I can get you out on bail."

"But..." CoCo could hear the hesitation in his voice.

"But, I don't want to go in front of a judge and get denied. I know a few that owe me a favor. Two of them are on vacation, and another one is occupied with a trial. So, when one becomes available that I can argue my case in front of, I'll get you out on bail."

"How long is that gonna take? I'm losing my mind being held up like an animal in this shit hole."

Mr. Katz wanted to say, "*Until your sister gives me the green light.*" But instead he said, "Be patient, it will happen soon," he lied.

"I'm counting on that. I know my sister has hit you off with a shit load of money to make sure I get the best defense. So I advise you to come through. She wouldn't be very happy if you didn't."

All the attorney could think to himself was, *If you only knew the truth!*

Chapter Seven
One Down, More To Go

After running into Arnez at the restaurant a few days ago, Denise felt it was time to give Delondo some pussy. The deal needed to be sealed. She had held out long enough to make him think she wasn't the drop-your-panties-hussy-for-a-dollar trick that she really was.

"I know you said you have to be to work early in the morning, so I'll go ahead and take you home," Delondo said, standing up from the couch. They had just finished watching "Menace to Society", a movie they both never got tired of. Lying on the couch looking at movies, doing some kissing and grinding had become a normal routine for them. And what would normally follow was Denise putting a halt to the foreplay and him taking her home. But not tonight.

"Baby, I'm not ready to go home."

"What, you want to watch another movie?"

"No, I want us to pretend like we're making our own."

"Huh…what you mean?"

"What do you think I mean? Don't you think we've waited long enough? Or don't you want the pussy anymore?" Denise straight witnessed his dick grow in less than five seconds. That shit was practically fighting to get out his jeans.

"Yo, I been wanting you, but I understood you wanted to wait, and I respected you for that."

"I don't want to wait no more. You've been such a gentleman and proven you deserve the goods, and I want you to have it."

"Damn, baby, that shit sound good like a motherfucker!"

Denise stood up and slipped out of her denim shorts and tank top. She had already planned on giving up the ass tonight, so she came prepared, wearing a sexy red, lace bra and panty set.

"I ain't know you had all that going on under your clothes," he said, admiring the full breasts and phat ass Denise was packing on her petite frame.

Delondo instantly zoomed in on her hardened nipples, taking them in his mouth. While one hand cupped her breast, the other one was sliding her panties to the side so his fingers could feel her wet juices. He tactfully stroked her clit for a few, getting her wetter. Once it felt as if he had her insides raining, he put one of his fingers in his mouth. "This pussy taste so good!" he moaned, lying Denise down on the couch and letting his tongue make love to her.

Denise was about to climb the walls because the nigga had her feeling so much pleasure, but she needed to get control over the situation. She had already decided that it was imperative that she put her freak game on Delondo. The plan was to get him pussy whipped. No matter how a nigga might try to front, she knew they all wanted a whore in the bed. It was cool to play all ladylike in the public, but if you brought that shit to the sheets, you were asking to have your man do an automatic trade-in.

Denise let Delondo eat her pussy for about five more minutes, and although it was killing her to change the position, she had a job to do, and her pleasure would have to wait so she could get a step closer to accomplishing her mission.

"Am I making you feel good, baby?" Delondo asked between finger and tongue fucking her.

"Yes, baby, but now I want to make you feel good." Denise seductively shifted her body and knelt down on the floor, sitting between Delondo's legs. She unbuckled his pants and pulled them down so quickly, he had no time to react. Before he knew it, his thick, long dick was resting peacefully in her mouth. Denise had Delondo exactly where she wanted him…by the balls.

*****

"Tech, why do you have to fuck wit' so many bitches? You constantly screaming that you don't want me dealing wit' no other niggas, but you stay runnin' up in new pussy!" Monica hissed, rolling her eyes, neck, hip and anything else she could move.

"Chill wit' all that riffing. Don't I look out for you? Whatever you need, don't I always come through? You ain't had to pay a bill since you started fuckin' wit' me, and that's why I dare you to fuck wit' another nigga. I don't need you to pay none of my shit, so our roles in this relationship are different…you dig?"

Monica stared at Tech's tall, chocolate fine black ass, and wanted to jump on him and beat the dog shit out of his trifling butt, but she knew it wouldn't make a damn difference in his behavior. He would continue to do whatever he wanted, and fuck whoever. No matter if Monica didn't approve.

"So it's like that. Tech, you're going to keep doing you no matter how much that shit fuck wit' me?"

"Baby, what do you want me to say? I love pussy…I can't help myself. But you my shorty. I'ma always hold you down, but you gon' have to stop bringing all this drama every other day. It is what it is."

"Whatever, Tech! But you better be careful. You keep chasing all that pussy, you gon' find yourself in some serious bullshit."

"Don't worry about me. I always got shit under control. You just stay in line, and that means checkin' that smartass mouth of yours," Tech advised as he picked up his car keys.

"You leaving? Where you going?"

"Baby, I got business to handle."

"You mean bitches to screw!"

"Here you go, bringing the drama. Didn't we just go over this? Women are hard-headed. Then, when a nigga don't come home, you act like you don't know why."

"Fuck you, Tech! Gon' head and hound down these ho's! I hope one of those bitches bite your dick off!" Monica screamed out before Tech slammed the door. She picked up the bottle of Heineken he was drinking and threw it against the door. "I hate you!" That was the problem. She didn't hate Tech. Monica fucked around not following her own rules, and let herself fall hard for a drug dealer who was a player and not thinking about her ass.

When Tech got outside, he noticed a woman with some of the nicest pair of legs he had ever seen standing by his car. His eyes roamed up until they landed on the ridiculous ass she had to go with them. He started having visions of bending her over and twisting her back out right there in the dead of the night.

"Yo, ma, can I help you wit' something?" Tech questioned, walking right up on the woman. He was surprised when she turned around. She was pretty as fuck too. *Damn, this bitch got the entire package. Yeah, I'ma have to add her to my collection of broads,* he thought to himself.

"Is this your car?"

"Yeah, why?

"I'm so sorry, but when I was backing out, I accidently hit it. I was checking to see if there's any damage. I apologize. It was an accident."

Tech walked over, pretending to thoroughly check for damage, when in reality, he could give a flying fuck if the whole fender was bent in. Getting the pussy would cover any damage. "I do see a dent right here."

"I saw that too, but I wasn't sure if it was already there."

"Nah, you did this."

"Please don't call the police to fill out an accident

report. I don't have any car insurance."

"So what, you want to pay for the damage out of pocket? 'Cause you have to fix this."

"I'm between jobs right now, and my money is tight. Can I make payments?"

"Baby girl, I'm not running a charity over here. You need to pay with some cash, or come up with another way to compensate me." Tech calmly bit down on his bottom lip, letting the woman know what was up.

"What do you want me to do?"

"What can you do?"

"It's up to you. You holding all the cards."

"You right, I am. Get in the car." Tech hit the switch to unlock the doors to his big body Benz. He couldn't believe his luck that some prime pussy had fallen into his lap like that, and he planned to take full advantage of it.

"You have a nice car," the woman said, closing the passenger door.

"I know, and you can ride in it sometimes if you act right." Tech wasted no time letting it be known what he wanted. "To begin working off your debt, you can start with sucking my dick," he said, unbuttoning his pants to pull out his dick.

"Before I start sucking you off, don't you even want to know my name?"

"We got plenty of time to exchange names. Right now, I want you to suck my dick. But if it'll make you feel better, knock yourself out and tell me your name."

"Chanel. And Arnez told me to tell you hello."

Before Tech could utter a word, Chanel had reached for the gun she had discreetly placed in the back of her waist, and blasted one bullet straight through Tech's head, splattering his brains on the driver's side glass window.

"That's one man down. And soon there won't be anyone left standing to protect you, Delondo," Chanel reasoned out loud as she got out of the car and jumped in hers before speeding off. Leaving Tech dead with his dick hanging out in full view.

Chapter Eight
Unravelling The Truth

Genesis remained in deep thought during his ride. The drive from Malibu to Beverly Hills wasn't a short one, but it was necessary.

The same driver who picked him up from the airport was now taking him to his destination. He was a trusted member of Quentin's team, and his assignment was to strictly accommodate any of Genesis' needs.

Upon finally reaching their destination, the black SUV pulled into the underground garage. The area was pretty much completely isolated, but with the dark tinted windows, there was no way anyone would be able to see who was inside.

"Yeah, and believe me, if he had gotten a divorce, that shit would be on every single urban blog you could think of. But come to think of it, he has been keeping a very low profile lately."

"What do you mean?"

"We both live in Beverly Hills, and run in the same circles. I usually see him out a few times a month. But now that I'm thinking about it, that hasn't been the case these last few months. I figured he was traveling, maybe overseas handling some business."

"Or maybe he's having problems with his wife and he's creeping with this other woman, but left town to keep shit on the low."

"That's a very good possibility."

"Do you know his wife's name?"

"No, but that's easy to find out. I'll also ask around to see who's been in touch with him. But I need to know before I do so, that the girl's father isn't trying to do some foul shit to Supreme, because I can't be a part of that."

"No, please ease your mind. He's simply concerned and wants to make sure that she's safe. I wouldn't even get you caught up in anything like that."

"Then I'm on it. Somebody has to have an idea where he is. Supreme is huge in this business and orchestrating way too many power moves to vanish. He has to be communicating on a regular with his key people. I'll have something for you soon."

"Cool. Thanks for looking out."

"Like I said, ain't no problem. But let me ask you, how long you plan on being on the run? That shit has to be taking a toll on you."

"Ain't that the truth!" Genesis sighed. "I finally got an attorney, and hopefully, he can get me out this shit."

"Since you have an attorney, you don't want to turn yourself in and maybe try to get a bail?"

"I can't do that and take the risk of bail being denied. I have too much shit to handle out here in these streets. The main thing is finding out who killed Deuce. Whoever took my man out has to pay with their life."

"I understand that, homey, but watch yourself. There's a very good chance that whoever killed your partner may want to take you out too."

"I know. That's why I have to find them before they find me."

"Just be careful," T-Roc warned. "But I'm on this. And if you need anything else from me, let me know."

"I will. It was good seeing you."

"You too, man." The two men tapped their fists on top of each other's before T-Roc got out the car.

Genesis felt somewhat better after meeting with him. He really wanted to find Maya. He felt it was the least he could do, since Quentin had done so much for him. With T-Roc on the case, he believed the probability of that happening was very much in his favor.

*****

When Talisa heard a knock at the door, she wondered who it could be. At first she was going to ignore it, not being in the mood for any visitors, but her curiosity got the best of her. She looked through the peephole, and although she easily identified the face, she was surprised to see her.

"Hi, Tonya. What brings you by?" Talisa asked after opening the door. She hadn't seen or talked to her since Deuce's funeral, and even then, their conversation was brief. The two women had never been friends, only mere acquaintances, since their boyfriends were best friends.

"Hey, Talisa, can I come in?"

"Sure." Talisa shut the door and led Tonya into the living room. "Can I get you anything to drink?"

"No, I'm fine. I'm not fine really, but…" Tonya's voice began to crack and tears welled up in her eyes.

Talisa didn't know if she should go comfort her with a hug, or let her be. She didn't know much about Tonya, except that before Deuce died, they got engaged and she was very much in love with him. "Let me get you something to wipe your eyes." Talisa went in the bathroom and got some tissue, then went back to Tonya, who was now in full blitz cry mode.

"I'm sorry, it wasn't my intention to come over here and break down crying. I wanted to know if you've been in touch with Genesis."

Talisa now wanted to break down and cry after hearing Tonya say his name, but she stayed strong. She figured it would do no good for both women to fall apart. "No, I haven't heard from him. I'm starting to wonder if I ever will."

"I'm sorry. I know how hard that must be for you."

"More than you know, especially since I'm carrying his child." The words slipped out so fast that by the time Talisa realized what she said, it was too late.

"You're pregnant? Does Genesis know?"

"No, nobody does but my doctor, and now you. But pretty soon I won't be able to hide it anyway," Talisa said, rubbing her stomach.

"How far along are you?"

"I'm in the early part of my second trimester."

"You're so small."

"I know. I have to start taking better care of myself and eating more. But I've been so depressed since Genesis left. I regret that I didn't tell him I was pregnant, because maybe then he wouldn't of left."

"You knew before he left?"

"Yep, I had just found out and wanted to surprise him, but then Deuce got killed, and CoCo called letting him know that they had been indicted and that the Feds could be coming to get him at any time. The next thing I know, I wake up, and he's gone. There is so much I didn't get to tell him. I've been praying every day that that he would call… but nothing. That's why I won't move, because if he comes back, I don't want him to have any problem finding me."

"For your sake and the baby's, I hope Genesis does come back. I also want him to come back for my own selfish reasons. I want him to find out who killed Deuce and get payback."

Talisa put her head back on the couch and closed her eyes for a brief second. She wasn't sure if it was in her best interest to reveal certain information to Tonya, but then another part of her felt she had the right to know.

"Tonya, I have something to tell you, but I need for you to keep it to yourself. It's for your own protection."

"What is it?"

"It's about Deuce."

"What about Deuce?"

Talisa could hear the rise in Tonya's voice. "I know who murdered him."

"What?" Tonya jumped up out of her seat. "You

know who killed Deuce and you ain't gone to the police!"

"It's not that simple."

"Yes the hell it is! Tell me who the fuck killed my fiancé!"

"Tonya, I understand that you're upset, but would you please calm down? You're making me regret that I'm even confiding in you."

Tonya took a few deep breaths and sat back down. She didn't want to fuck this up. Since the day Deuce died, she had nightmares, and it all centered around not knowing who killed her baby. She wasn't going to let getting over-emotional keep her from learning the truth. "I apologize. I shouldn't have screamed at you."

"You have every right to be upset, but trust me, we both have to try and remain calm. We're dealing with some dangerous people, and the only reason I didn't tell you sooner was because I don't want to put your life in jeopardy."

"Please, tell me who it is. I promise to keep it to myself until you tell me otherwise."

"A man named Arnez, my ex-boyfriend, is the person who is responsible for the murder of Deuce and Antwon."

"Why would your ex-boyfriend want to kill them?"

"Genesis was the intended target, but whoever Arnez hired, fucked the job up and killed the wrong people."

Tonya put her head down, completely stunned. Mistaken identity mixed with being at the wrong place at the wrong time is what ended the life of the man she loved. Tonya always thought that once she found out the truth about what happened to Deuce, she would feel better, but instead, she felt worse. He was never even the intended victim. She couldn't blame it on some rival drug dealer who was jealous because of the money Deuce was making or the car he was driving…it wasn't even about him. To Tonya, that seemed to make his demise that much more tragic.

"Does Genesis know any of this?" Tonya asked.

"No, and that's why I need to talk to him. I have to warn him. Arnez isn't going to give up. He knows that Genesis is very much alive, and he won't be satisfied until he's dead."

"Do you have any idea where Arnez is now?"

"I'm assuming he went back to Atlanta. But I really don't know. I'm just praying he stays far away from me."

Talisa may have wanted never to see Arnez's face again, but Tonya was praying for the exact opposite. If she had to get on a plane to Atlanta and track Arnez down, that's what she would do. One way or another, she was determined to make sure Arnez met the same fatal fate that he put on Deuce.

Chapter Nine
Death Wish

"I can't believe Tech is dead." Monica had been repeating that exact same line all morning. It was as if she was in sort of trance.

"I can't believe he was found with his dick hanging out right in front of our apartment building! I mean, was the nigga getting head in his car right outside our front door? Damn, he trifling!" Denise spit, looking through the blinds. The cops had been outside since early in the morning when somebody discovered Tech's dead body.

When Delondo was dropping Denise off the next morning after they spent the night together, they arrived to a lot full of police cars. At first they both thought a drug bust had went down, but then they noticed the yellow tape and figured out there had been a murder. Little did they know, it was Tech about to be carried off in a body bag.

Delondo was the first to notice Tech's Benz, and he wouldn't of thought anything of it considering Tech fucked with Monica, but the slumped over body with his brain splattered on the driver's window, and his dick making a cameo appearance made it evident that shit was not sweet. Delondo was completely devastated, but it didn't compare to the hysterics Monica put on when Denise woke her up to give her the bad news.

Monica ran out of the apartment damn near halfway naked, not believing the man killed was Tech. She demanded to see the body, causing a scene that looked to be straight out of a 'hood movie.

Now, here they were a couple of hours later, and Monica had finally stabilized, but she kept repeating the same damn sentence, and it was working Denise's last nerve.

"Who did this to him, and why?" Monica asked, finally saying something different which thrilled the hell out of Denise.

"I don't know, but I'll tell you one thing, Delondo is sure gonna find the fuck out. He is beyond heated. I knew the two of them were close, but I had no idea that they were that close. He taking that shit hard."

"Yeah, Tech handled a majority of Delondo's business, so you know he had to not only trust him, but be close."

"Well, Delondo don't really discuss his business dealings with me, so I don't know who he's close to."

"Tech constantly ran off at the mouth, especially about Delondo. He had mad respect for him and his hustle."

"I didn't know Tech like that, but that's fucked up he's dead. Plus, you my girl, and I know how much you was diggin' dude."

"Don't none of that shit matter now. We already know how this game can be played out, and getting killed is forever an option. My thing is, damn, why the fuck did it have to be with a nigga I caught feelings for?"

Fuck catching feelings! I hope you caught and saved some serious chips from that nigga. Shit, it's gon' take you a minute to find and break another motherfucker in to start hittin' you off with some cash. Until then, I better put some extra work in on Delondo, 'cause one of us gotta hold this situation down. Neither one of us got the type of job that's bringing in no real income. You held it down for me when my paper was dried up, least I can do is the same for you, Denise thought as she watched a single tear roll down Monica's face.

*****

Ring…Ring…Ring

Tonya looked over at the clock and wondered who could be calling her this early in the morning. She put a pillow over her head trying to ignore it, but the phone kept ringing. She glimpsed at the caller ID, but it read "Private".

"Hello," she mumbled into the phone, still half asleep.

"Yo, why you got your cell turned off? I need to come over there."

"'Cause I'm sleep. If I knew you would call me on my home phone, I would've turned the ringer off."

"Chill! I wouldn't of called like this if it wasn't important."

"What's up?"

"Tech got killed last night."

Hearing that information quickly woke Tonya out of being half sleep. "Delondo, get the fuck outta here! Do you know who did it?"

"No, but get up, I'm on my way over."

He hung up before Tonya could even respond, but she wasn't surprised. Ever since she could remember, her cousin had been like that.

Everything was about him. He felt a person's world was supposed to begin and stop around him, and most of the time it did. It was hard to tell Delondo no, and it wasn't only because he had a shit load of money, but he was also very generous with it. That combination made just about everybody kiss his ass.

Tonya dragged herself out of bed and jumped into the shower. She didn't know how far away Delondo was, but she figured he would be at her apartment sooner rather than later.

While in the shower, all she thought about was Tech being dead. She had known him for a few years now, and he and Delondo were super close. So she wasn't shocked that he wanted to come over. He probably needed somebody to talk to.

Not more than ten minutes after Tonya threw on some clothes, Delondo was at her door. "I'm so sorry," Tonya said, giving her cousin a hug.

"Yo, I just can't believe my man is dead. Yesterday I was laughing wit' this nigga, and now I'ma have to start making funeral arrangements."

"What happened?"

"I don't know all the details yet. What I do know is that somebody blew his brains out while he was sitting in his car."

"Where was he?"

"An apartment parking lot of some broad he was fucking with."

"Damn! Tech was good people. Does Fatima know?"

"No, I didn't call her yet. You know she's on West Coast time, and I didn't want to wake the baby. Fuck! I can't believe his son's gon' have to grow up without his father!" Delondo said, shaking his head.

"I know. Fatima's gon' take that shit hard. He fucked around a lot and put her through hell, but she loved that nigga."

"And all that fuckin' around might of got his ass killed."

"Why do you say that?"

"Because he was found dead in his car with his pants down. Did some jealous boyfriend walk up on them and see their girlfriend giving him head? I'm speculating, but it don't seem drug related."

"Tech was too damn careless when it came to fucking with these chicks. He was at the apartment complex of one female he was dealing with, then you think he was getting head in his car from some other female? That's just sloppy. But he still didn't deserve to die."

"I don't give a damn what he done! That's my motherfuckin' folk, and I loved that nigga to death! That ain't no motherfuckin' joke! Whoever did this shit is going the fuck down…I promise you that!"

Tonya didn't doubt that shit for a minute.

Knowing her cousin, he would probably handle that shit like a "Cops" tip hotline and offer a handsome reward for any information about the murder. But instead of the tip leading to an arrest, it would lead to the murder of the perpetrator.

*****

"I know Delondo's somewhere sick right now," Arnez said to Chanel as they lay in bed.
"You should've seen his face when I mentioned your name. He knew right then his time was up, and was helpless to do a damn thing about it," Chanel laughed, finding humor in her role in Tech's death. She didn't think twice about pulling the trigger and ending the existence of another human being. His life was as meaningless and simple to her as stepping on an ant and then wiping it off the bottom of her shoe.
"I can only imagine. But make sure you give all of them the same message before ending their lives. I want them to know their death is courtesy of me—especially Delondo. That smug fuck makes me ill. New York niggas have no respect. They come on the scene without any regards to protocol. Delondo will regret the day he ever decided to strong-arm my territory. Soon, he'll be

wishing he kept his arrogant ass in NYC."

"That's right, baby, and it's gonna be my pleasure to make that shit happen for you. I have to go out of town for a couple of days, but when I get back, I'll go right down the list until Delondo and his entire crew are out of commission."

"Where are you going?"

"I have to go visit CoCo."

"That's smart. You don't want her to start getting suspicious."

"Exactly. The attorney went to see her, now it's my turn. How long do you want her to stay locked up before I have the attorney try to get her out on bail?"

"How long is it going to take you to convince her to retire from the game for good and turn all her connections over to me…mainly, Quentin Jacobs?"

"That depends. From what the attorney told me, she and Genesis both might walk. The whole jail experience might be enough for CoCo to retire from the drug game, but if so, I promise you, she's going to turn over all her connects to Genesis. Which means Quentin will be dealing with him and nobody else."

"Then we have to make sure that doesn't happen. That's just more reason to get rid of Genesis once and for all. A dead man can't make deals."

Trust No One

"I ain't never been so happy to see you in my entire life! I've missed you!" CoCo exclaimed.

"I've missed you too. Sorry I'm just now coming to see you, but you know how hectic shit's been."

"I can imagine, especially with me being in here you got to handle everything on your own. But after speaking with my attorney, I have a feeling I'll be coming home a lot sooner than I thought."

"Yeah, he mentioned that with homeboy out the picture, things are looking up for you."

"Exactly!" CoCo smiled. "That was the best news I heard since I got to this motherfucker."

"So, how is shit up in here? Ain't nobody fuckin' with you, are they?"

"Nope. Besides a few chicks being coupled up, everybody pretty much keeps to themselves. You have a few fights here and there, but for the most part, shit is low key. But this shit ain't for me."

"You look good. I like your hair short like that."

"Shit, I ain't got no fuckin' choice. And nobody's doing weaves up in this motherfucker," CoCo joked.

"Glad you ain't lost your sense of humor. But on the real, your face is so pretty you don't need all that hair. Looking at your shit has me seriously contemplating taking this weave out and getting my hair cut short."

"At least you got a choice."

"Don't worry, soon you'll be having choices too. This lawyer is supposed to be the business. Arnez referred him to me."

"He must be official then, 'cause Arnez don't fuck with no slackers. How is he doing anyway? Is he still in Atlanta?"

"He's good. When I told him I was coming to see you, he told me to tell you hello. But we're in Philly now."

"*We're?* Are you fucking around with Arnez?"

"No, of course not! I didn't mean it like that. You know ATL is hot right now, so I'm helping him make some moves in Philly."

"I had no idea you been in Philly. How long have you've been there?"

"Not that long, maybe a few weeks."

"When are you going back to Atlanta?"

"When things cool down."

"I see."

"Well, I better be going. I see the guards are starting to let us know that visitation time is up."

"Yeah, the time flew by. But I'm glad you came. When are you coming to see me again?"

"Soon, I promise."

"I'm glad to hear that. We're family. No, we're more than that; we're twins. No bond is stronger than that of a twin—right?"

"No doubt. We've always had each other's backs, and we always will. I'll see you soon."

CoCo stood up and watched her sister walk away. She wanted to push this sick feeling that had come over her away, but something wouldn't let her, and it was called "gut instinct". CoCo could read her sister better than anybody, and she should because they had always been in each other's shadow. That's why she knew her sister was lying to her about Arnez. And CoCo wanted to know why her sister lied about it, and how long had they been fucking around, because there was no doubt in her mind that they were fucking.

What are you hiding, Chanel? Clearly you have gotten so comfortable with the nigga that you slipped and used the term 'we're' like you all are some type of couple. You tried to play the shit off, but it was too late.

Your cover was blown. I can always tell when you're lying, but it's always to somebody else, never me. But how the fuck did you get wrapped up with Arnez, and why are you trying to keep it from me? That's my question. But damn, something is telling me I ain't gonna like the answer, CoCo thought as she headed back to her cell.

*****

Genesis kept glancing at his cell phone, wrestling with whether he should call Talisa or not. He knew it wasn't a good idea, but not being able to see her was eating him up. Constantly staring at her picture was losing its luster…he needed more. He was more than a hundred percent sure that the Feds had her phone tapped, so he would have to keep the call brief and not say too much, if anything.

Genesis dialed Talisa's number, and it just rang. Right when he was about to hang up, she answered.

"Hello." The sweetness of her voice sent chills down his spine. "Hello, is anybody there?" Then there was a pause in Talisa's voice. "Who is this… Genesis, is that you?"

Genesis was stunned for a second that she

thought it was him on the phone. But then he knew how deep their love was, and with that sort of bond you could sometimes feel things that the average person couldn't.

"Baby, I know it's you. Please answer me! I have to speak to you! You're in danger, and I'm not talking about the Feds."

The temptation to communicate with Talisa had Genesis' mind in overdrive. As he opened his mouth to confirm what Talisa believed, his better judgment kicked in and he hung up the phone.

"Oh, baby, I'm so sorry I had to be selfish, but I couldn't go any longer without hearing your voice. Knowing I was on the other end of the phone and for me not to speak had to crush you. Forgive me, baby."

Genesis sat down on his bed and held the last picture that he and Talisa took together. He remembered them being so happy. He took his index finger and glided it over her face, reminiscing on the smoothness of her skin and every curve on her body and how the warmth of her insides always soothed his soul.

As his mind began to drift deeper into his thoughts of Talisa, the ring of his cell phone jolted him out his thoughts.

"Yo, I was beginning to think you abandoned the project," Genesis said, when he answered the phone.

"Nah, man, finding out the information was a tad bit harder than I thought it would be, but I got something for you."

"Spill."

"From what I understand, Supreme sold his crib in Beverly Hills and moved to Miami. I don't know if it was a permanent move, but from all indications, he's been there for at least a couple of months."

"Really! Is his wife with him?"

"Not sure. But I did find out her name. It's Precious Cummings. I mean it *was* Cummings. Now it's Precious Mills."

"Miami…you sure about that?"

"I had my people dig and double dig, and that's what they all came up with. I believe it's accurate. I even have an address for you."

"I owe you big time, T-Roc."

"Damn sure do, and don't forget it."

After Genesis jotted down the information, he hung up with T-Roc, and without delay, placed a call to Quentin. This was the sort of break Genesis had been anticipating, and he was pleased to be the one to deliver. Now all he needed to know was if his services on the matter were complete, or would his next stop be Miami.

Chapter Eleven
Watching You

Arnez was sitting in the back of his chauffer driven car, resorting to his now customary stalking of Talisa. He had one of his henchmen monitoring her movements daily, and at least once a week he would personally participate in watching her comings and goings. Arnez got some sort of sick thrill being able to track her every move. But watching was no longer giving him the satisfaction he needed. He wanted to make contact. He had to let Talisa know he was invading on her space, and that there was no escaping him.

After Talisa left the doctor's office, she was

mentally exhausted. She was trying to remain strong for the sake of the baby, but she was losing the battle. And the fact that she knew in her heart that it was Genesis on the other end of the phone the other day wasn't helping her cause. She needed his support now more than ever. Talisa wished she had blurted out that she was pregnant. If that didn't make Genesis come back to her, then she knew nothing would.

Arnez stared intently as Talisa left her doctor's office, but he was concerned. For the last couple of months he watched her go to her appointments, but instead of gaining weight, she seemed to be fading away. He couldn't detect the slightest bulge in her stomach which worried him. If, in fact, she was carrying his baby like he hoped, then he wanted a healthy child.

Arnez had his driver trail behind Talisa as she drove off in her black Aston Martin. When she reached her high-rise and pulled underneath into the garage, they followed. They kept their distance and waited as Talisa parked her car and then walked towards the elevator.

"Cut her off," Arnez ordered his chauffer. The driver sped up, completely catching Talisa off guard as the car cornered her in.

The loud screech that emerged as the driver

quickly pushed down on the brakes frightened the crap out of Talisa. Her body jerked back, causing her to drop her car keys. She bent down to retrieve them, and then at the same time, quickly tried to figure out an escape. But the way the car was angled, she had little room to move.

"No need to be scared," Arnez announced, stepping out of the car, making Talisa's heart freeze.

"What the hell are you doing here, Arnez?"

"Is that any way to greet someone you share such a long history with?"

"Our history isn't long, it's just tainted. Now, please have your driver move this car so I can go about my business."

"You know I can't do that. I haven't seen you in what seems like a lifetime. We have so much to catch up on."

"Oh, you mean how two innocent men died all due to your jealousy of Genesis? And once I tell the police what you did, the only thing you'll be talking about is how many years you'll be spending in the state prison."

"My dear Talisa, if you were going to speak with the police, you would've already done so. But what would you say without sounding delusional? 'My ex-boyfriend called, and told me he was about to have someone kill my boyfriend, who is now on the run from the Feds'? You need more people."

"It doesn't matter, because Genesis' knows," she lied, hoping to plant, if only a drop of fear in Arnez's evil heart. "And I promise you, he will get payback for what happened to his best friend. Not to mention that when he finds out you're harassing me, he's really going to hunt you down."

"I find it admirable that a woman in your condition is trying to appear to be so strong, but you forget, I know you, Talisa. You're this close," Arnez lifted up his hand, putting a small space between his thumb and forefinger, "to totally falling apart and with the problems Genesis has to deal with right now. You're the last person he's thinking about saving. He's too busy trying to save himself."

"Leave now, Arnez, or I'll call the police. I'm sure with the life you live, they'll be able to come up with something to arrest you for."

"Is that anyway to talk to the man who might be the father of your unborn child?"

"You're crazier than I thought."

"And you're more of an idiot than I thought if you don't know that the only reason I haven't killed you yet is because I believe that there's a slight possibility the baby you're carrying could be mine."

"You're the worse kind of monster," Talisa said, shaking her head in disgust.

"And you don't think Genesis is? He's a killer

just like me. But you better pray I am the father of that child, because at least I'll be around to raise it. Genesis is either going to end up dead or in jail. Not very good options for you."

"Any option is better than having to see your face! Now stay the fuck away from me or I'll kill you myself!"

"I'll leave for now, because I don't want to upset you, you know, for the baby's sake, but I will be back. And you need to eat. You look like shit. I'll be very upset if my child isn't born healthy because its mother was too stupid to take care of herself."

When Arnez got back in the car and they drove off, Talisa succumbed to all the anger, fear and frustration she tried her best to conceal in front of Arnez. Her hands were shaking to the point that she could barely hit the 'up' button on the elevator.

"This can't be happening to me!" Talisa muttered as she stood in the elevator, fidgeting with the buttons, briefly forgetting what floor she lived on. It was one thing for her to have to deal with not having Genesis around, but adding Arnez into the mix was way too much for her to handle. Her legs were weak and she could barely hold herself up. All she wanted to do was make it to her apartment and lay down before she passed out.

When the elevator doors opened, Talisa struggled down the hallway, which seemed much longer to her than usual. Her vision began to get blurry, and she had to use the wall to hold herself up. As she got closer to the entry of her apartment door, she could see what appeared to be a tall man standing there. But by this point, she was almost blind and couldn't decipher if she really did see a man or if she was hallucinating.

No longer able to stand up, Talisa reached out her arms and prayed someone was there, because if not, she was about to hit the floor head first.

*****

"Genesis, I had faith you would come through for me and you have."

"I told you I would, but don't get too optimistic. Even though we've tracked down Supreme, it doesn't mean your daughter is with him. And like I expected, he's married."

"Supreme has a wife?"

"Yes, her name is Precious Cummings, and they share a daughter together."

"Precious Cummings…why does that name sound so familiar to me?" Quentin wondered.

"Not too long ago they went through a very public ordeal with the kidnapping of their daughter. Maybe you heard her name then."

"Maybe so, but it doesn't matter that he's married. I still believe Maya is with him. I don't know what's going on with his wife, but the last time I saw Mike, he told me Maya was living in Beverly Hills with this music mogul, Supreme."

"And there's only one Supreme that fits that description, so he had to be talking about him."

"But there's only one way to find out."

"Does that mean you're going to use the address I gave you and head to Miami?"

"I could, but I would prefer if you did it."

"I have no problem with that, but is there a reason why you don't want to go?"

"As I told you, Maya has no idea I'm her father. I'm a complete stranger to her. I'm not interested in disrupting her life, but I want to make sure she's okay."

"Does that mean you're never going to tell her the truth?"

"I don't have any intentions of doing so. If she's safe and happy, there's no need to. But of course if she needs anything, especially financial support, then I'll give it to her…whatever she needs."

"So, all you want me to do is go to Miami and make sure she's okay, not talk to her or anything."

"Only if she seems like she might be in some kind of trouble."

"I got you. So, when do you want me to leave?"

"Immediately. I'll get you a ticket, and if all goes

well, you'll be there no longer than a couple of days. As soon as you return, I want you to meet with your attorney. He's already begun working on the case. He told me that CoCo has an attorney whose name is Robert Katz. He's supposed to be very good at what he does."

"That's good to hear. I worry about CoCo. I hate that she's been locked up for all these months. I wonder what took so long for her to get counsel."

"I wondered the same thing. I know CoCo has a lot of money, and even if the Feds got a hold of it like they did yours, Chanel has access to ton of money too. And if she didn't, Chanel knows she could've come to me. So I have no idea what was going on. I'm just glad things finally seem to be coming together for CoCo. Besides hardened and sick criminals, jail ain't a place for anybody to be, especially a woman."

"I feel you on that. There are things that are fucked up about me from spending years in a juvenile detention. 'Til this day, I wonder where my mother and my sister are."

"I had no idea you weren't in contact with your family. Have you tried to look for them?"

"That was the first thing I did when I got out, but it was like they vanished off the face of this earth. I still carry around a picture we took the last time I saw them. I've only seen my baby sister once, but I remember her vividly. Her name was

Genevieve. I would give anything to have them back in my life."

"Then you will. It's a big world, but if you try hard enough, you can locate anybody. Let's get you out of this drug bullshit with the Feds, and then focus on finding your mother and sister."

"That's what's up!" Genesis grinned. "But for now, Miami, here I come!"

Chapter Twelve
My Enemy, Your Enemy

The flat screen television mounted on the kitchen wall was on, but Delondo seemed to be looking through it and not at it.

Denise stood over the stove scrambling some eggs, wondering how long this gloomy spell would be in effect. It carried over from one crib to another. There was no escaping it. She would go home and have to endure it with Monica, and then come over to Delondo's crib and tolerate it with him. During some peaks of aggravation, Denise thought maybe Monica and Delondo needed to hook up so they could commiserate together.

"Baby, you sure you don't want some eggs? I

cooked plenty." There was dead silence, which had become typical. Denise would've thought Delondo turned mute if it wasn't for the fact he would say a few words during sex. That seemed to be the only time he would speak, or when Tech's name was brought up.

"I know you had a funeral for Tech in LA. Are you going to do something for him here in Philly?" Denise could care less. She was only trying to get the motherfucker to use his words.

"No, he ain't got no *real* friends in Philly. All his folks were at the funeral in Cali."

"There were people here who had love for him."

"Like who?"

"Monica! How soon we forget," Denise mocked.

"Not to shit on your homegirl, but she was one of many bitches Tech fucked with. His only certified girl is in LA, raising their son. So if your girl caught them type of feelings for him, she was playing herself."

Denise got hot when Delondo said that shit. She couldn't help but think about her previous relationship with Genesis and how she fell in love with him, but she was nothing more than some passing through pussy to him. Monica knew that Tech had a girl, a baby, and a few other chicks he fucked with, but she also thought they shared something special, that she meant something to him. But in case Denise assumed otherwise,

Delondo made sure to set the record straight.

"So, is that what I am to you, one of your many bitches?"

"How did this become about us?"

"You went there about Monica and Tech. It made me question what the situation is for us."

"I dig you, or I wouldn't have you up in my crib, but we're still getting to know each other. We'll see what happens."

"I need to be going. I'ma call me a cab."

"Wait! You leaving? Why?"

"I have some things to do. I'll call you later."

"Wait. You don't have to call a cab. I'll take you home."

"Whatever you want to do," Denise said with indifference in her tone. "I'ma get my stuff together."

While Delondo drove her home, Denise didn't speak a word to him. She felt flipping the script was exactly what he needed. First, he was giving her the silent treatment, then when he decided to turn up the volume, he took a jab at her best friend. Then when she asked him about their relationship, he gave some casual 'we are getting to know each other' shit. Denise had been burned enough times to know not to waste her time on a man that wasn't really interested.

When they pulled up in front of her apartment,

Denise grabbed her stuff to get out. "Thanks for the ride."

"That's all you have to say?"

"What do you want me to say?"

"Listen, I know I've been in a fucked up mood lately, but you know I'm going through some shit. You have to understand that."

"I would understand more if you would talk to me and tell me what's going on. I had no idea you were so close to Tech. You never even spoke about him."

"I put people in my life in groups and I separate them. I only discuss individuals that are within their particular group. Tech wasn't in your group, so I had no reason to talk about him with you."

"I see. So again, I'm trying to figure out what group I fit in, and how many are in it."

"If you're asking am I seeing other women, yes. But are you special to me? The answer is yes to that too. And no, I'm not like Tech, who juggles multiple women on any given day. I take the female company I keep much more serious than that. All I'm saying is that I want to see what can happen between us. I know you might've been put off by what I said earlier, and I apologize. I'm working through some shit, but I want you to be there while I'm getting through it. Will you do that for me?"

"Of course. That's all I want."

"Good. So, can I come back and get you later on tonight?"

"I'd like that."

"Me too."

Denise leaned over and kissed Delondo. For the first time in forever, she finally felt a dude was digging her for real. Like there was a chance they could build a serious relationship that included more than great sex and tricking for a minute before trading her in for the next piece of ass.

"I'll see you later on," Denise smiled and got out the car. She waved as Delondo drove off. She was glad they were able to cut through the ice and get back on the right path.

She headed to her apartment with optimism looming in the air. The only other thing she wished would happen now, was for Monica to get back to her old self. She missed how they would kick it. Monica used to stay cracking jokes, and now she would barely crack a smile. But Denise was determined to change that right now.

"Girl, how about we go to your favorite restaurant today…my treat?" Denise said as soon as she opened the door. She assumed Monica would be posted up in the same spot in front of the television like she had been for the last few weeks.

"I wanted to call you, but dude wasn't having it," Monica groaned as she stood with her arms folded in front of her chest.

"Why are you in my apartment, and what do you want?" Denise looked over her shoulder making sure Delondo was gone, and slammed the door.

"I was expecting a much warmer reception from you, especially since I didn't blow your cover with your boyfriend."

"Arnez, you have some nerve coming to my crib! You used me, and Genesis almost died because of that shit!"

"But he didn't."

"Yeah, but two other people died in his place. I want you out, and don't ever come back!"

"This is a much different attitude than the one you had a few months ago when you gladly took my money."

"Yeah, that's because you were selling me the dream of helping you break up Talisa and Genesis so I could get him back, not no murder shit. I would've never been down for that, and I damn sure wouldn't have taken your money."

"It's too late. You did, and now I need you to do something else for me."

"I'll give you your twenty-five hundred dollars back. Just get the fuck out my crib and don't ever come back."

"How about you keep that money and add say, fifty-thousand to it."

"What the hell can I give you that is worth fifty-thousand dollars?" Denise was stunned by the amount. She was also curious and interested in Arnez's offer, because to her, fifty stacks was nothing to sneeze at.

"Help me bring down Delondo," Arnez replied casually.

"Excuse me…what the fuck! Get out!"

"Delondo is going down with or without your help. So, you can either help me and make some money, or not help me and lose him anyway."

"I'm not losing shit! Now, like I said, get the fuck out!"

"Once I enlighten Delondo about your sheisty behavior with Genesis, he'll return you like the damaged goods you are."

"I'll deny it. And I know you two are enemies, so he won't believe you."

"If you're willing to take that chance, then go right ahead. But I advise you to think about it very carefully. You have forty-eight hours to make your decision," Arnez informed Denise before walking to the door. "Oh, and ladies, enjoy your meal. It's on me," he said, tossing three bills on the floor.

"That nigga is no joke. Talk about a lose—lose situation…you're fucked!" Monica stood, shaking her head.

"This can't be happening!" Denise said, sitting down on the couch and putting her hands over her face.

"Yes the fuck it is. That nigga got balls."

"There has to be a way for me to get out of this shit."

"The only thing I can think of is lie and tell him you're willing to help, but then warn Delondo."

"But if I do that, Delondo is going to get mad suspicious and want to know how I found out, and what my relationship is with Arnez. I would have to tell him the truth about Genesis, and you know that nigga would stop fuckin' with me over that shit."

"Not necessarily. If you explain to him that Arnez basically tricked you, then he might understand. Yeah, he'll be a little pissed, but he might give you a pass. I mean it's not like you knew or wanted anybody to get killed. That crazy fuck, Arnez orchestrated all that shit, not you."

"I don't know, Monica. I'm scared. I'm really feeling Delondo and I think he's really feeling me too. I don't want to fuck this up."

"Then that's even more reason to come clean with him. If you all are really digging each other like that, then you'll get through it."

Delondo was pulling up in the parking lot and watched as Arnez came out of Denise's apartment. He slowed down and pulled his car over to the side, not wanting to be noticed. He sat for a few more minutes to see if Denise would come out, but she didn't. Arnez got in the back seat of an SUV and it drove off.

What the fuck was Arnez doing at Denise's apartment? They didn't act like they knew each other when we were at the restaurant. Maybe Monica just started fuckin' with him. I gotta think about this for a minute, Delondo thought to himself.

"I'll give this shit back to her later," he said, tossing Denise's cell phone on the passenger seat and driving off.

*****

Tonya was packing up the last few boxes of personal items at Tech's apartment to send to Fatima in Cali. Delondo asked her to do it because he said he didn't have the time. Tonya knew her cousin was extremely busy, but thought it had more to do with it being painful for him than anything else.

"Thank goodness Fatima didn't come here and get his shit," Tonya said out loud as she opened a drawer that was full of pictures he had of other women, including some who were butt ass naked. While tossing them in a nearby trashcan, one familiar face popped out. "I had no idea Tech was fucking with Monica." Tonya could tell the picture was sort of recent because of the hairstyle Monica had. It was the same cut she had when they saw each other at the nail salon. "Damn, it's a small world!" *I wonder how close they were, and if she was still fucking with him before he died. If so, she's probably feeling some kind of way about it. Maybe I should call her, or maybe go visit and see how she's doing,* Tonya thought to herself.

As Tonya was taping up her last box, she heard the front door opening. At first she got a little nervous, until she heard Delondo call out her name.

"I'm back here in his bedroom," Tonya called out.

"Yo, you did your thing in here. All his shit packed up?"

"You know I handle mine. I don't be wasting no time."

"Yeah, you don't."

"I'm surprised to see you here. I thought you weren't coming by until tomorrow to pick this stuff up."

"I was in the neighborhood so I decided to stop through," Delondo huffed before sitting down on the bed.

"You alright? You seem stressed. Is being in Tech's crib got you feeling some sort of way?"

"Nah, that's not it."

"Then what is it?"

"It's this girl I'm fuckin' with."

"Oh shit, let me find out some chick got my cousin open. I need to know who she is, 'cause you don't ever let me meet any of your girlfriends."

"You know I don't be having no girlfriends. They're more like close acquaintances."

"So why this one got you stressing?"

"This one might be a little more special, or at least I thought."

"Would you tell me what happened?"

"She spent the night with me last night, and when I dropped her off today, she left her phone in my car. I came back to give it to her, and I see this nigga, Arnez, who is my straight up enemy, coming out her crib."

Tonya's ears instantly widened when she heard the name 'Arnez'. It was only a few weeks ago that Talisa told her he was the person responsible for the murder of Deuce. Tonya had promised Talisa she wouldn't share the information with anybody, and although difficult, she had kept her word. "Did you confront her about it?"

"Not yet. I'm trying to calm down. I don't want to jump to any conclusions because the nigga could be fucking with her roommate."

"Roommate?"

"Yeah, she has a roommate, and maybe that's who Arnez was there to see. And it would make sense, because from the time I dropped her off and I came back, it was only a few minutes. So it would seem logical that he had already been there."

Tonya's mind was flipping through crazy thoughts. She thought about the picture she saw of Monica and Tech together. Then this chick Delondo was dealing with had a roommate and they lived in the neighborhood. Unless Denise and Monica moved recently, which Tonya doubted, they mos def lived around the area. There was only one way to confirm if her suspicions were accurate, even though she wanted to be wrong. Tonya decided to play it cool. The last thing she wanted her cousin to know was that she was fetching for answers, so she would have to pose her questions carefully.

"Yeah, you're probably right, and getting yourself all worked up for nothing. He probably is fucking with the roommate."

"True, but I still don't want her anywhere near that nigga. He's a sneaky ass snake."

"That might be difficult to maneuver since they live together. She can't tell her roommate who to date."

"True, I can't regulate what Monica does, but it's dead on that when it comes to Denise."

I can't believe Denise managed to get her claws into my cousin. Dude, I thought you were smarter than that. You must've fallen for that same innocent girl routine she keeps in rotation. But you grown, that's on you. Sooner or later you'll discover what a simple ass trick she is. Until then, I need to know which of them has dealings with Arnez, and why, Tonya thought to herself, determined to find out the truth.

Chapter Thirteen
Wanted

Genesis got off his flight to Miami feeling relaxed. With his authentic new driver's license and credit cards, it was like he had become a new person. He did remain cautious with his appearance, always wearing a baseball cap even though he let his hair grow out instead of keeping his signature bald head. No one seemed to notice him, but he was far from Philly where everyone knew he was a wanted man. Cali and Miami were both another world, and that suited Genesis just fine.

As he made his way through the airport, he went downstairs to the baggage claim area, where Quentin told him one of his drivers would be waiting for him outside. Genesis couldn't help but think that Quentin seemed to have an endless resource of people that were willing to do whatever he required of them. He looked forward to the day he got his life back on track, when he would have it like that too.

Genesis was welcomed by the bright Florida sun and wasted no time looking for the black tinted SUV which he noticed parked several feet away. He took a step forward, and then took off his shades. Before anybody could say a word, he dropped his bag and put his hands up.

"Get down on the ground, now!" one of the undercover officers yelled out. After that announcement, they seemed to come swarming out from every direction—several taxis, a couple of buses, and a few unmarked cars. He also saw the man who he assumed was there to pick him up getting tugged out of the SUV in handcuffs.

"Genesis Taylor, you have the right to remain silent…"

Genesis laid on the ground with his hands cuffed behind his back as the officer read him his rights. He wasn't even listening. Instead, he watched as the passersby gawked at him and whispered, trying to figure out who he was and what the fuck he had done. This shit was going down in Miami, so Genesis imagined they figured it had to be related to drugs. It was no secret that Miami did operate the largest cartels on the East Coast. He did find it hilarious that his business there had nothing to do with narcotics, but instead, to find a missing girl who would stay missing now that Genesis was caught and on his way to jail.

*****

"Where am I?" Talisa muttered, waking up hours later.

"You're in the hospital."

"What about my...."

"The baby is fine," her father said, quickly easing her mind.

"Daddy, what are you doing here? That was you who I saw standing outside my apartment door," Talisa said, remembering what happened.

"Yes, your mother and I were worried about you. Now I see we had great reason to be. Why didn't you tell us you were pregnant?"

Talisa turned her head away, not wanting to face her father. She didn't know how to tell him how ashamed she was. He had always had such high expectations of her, and once again, she had let him down.

"Talisa, are you going to answer me?"

"Not right now, Daddy. But I am glad you're

here. I need your support, more than you even realize."

*****

Chanel was parked in a nondescript car across from a project building in Southwest Philly. This was the third day she had been watching key members of Delondo's crew conduct business. This used to be the same project that Arnez had on lock, until Delondo had his people bulldoze their way in. But that was soon about to change.

The sun was beginning to set, and shortly like clockwork, they would begin dispersing into the lobby of one of the buildings. This was a routine of theirs, since the cops seemed to go harder and patrol the area more once it got dark.

Chanel wasn't in a rush. She had no problem waiting the men out. Her focus was making sure Arnez's orders would be carried out precisely to his liking, and she came prepared to do that. Once she completed her task, all the necessary damage would be done, and Delondo would no doubt get the message. But by then, it would be too late. The majority of his crew would be wiped out and he wouldn't have the resources to fight back.

Once the area cleared up and the crew headed

inside, Chanel drove around to the back of the building and parked in a deserted alley. Right on time, the dope fiend whose services she retained came walking up. Dressed in her signature all black, Chanel stepped out of the car to handle her business.

"I see you brought it, and it's still hot…perfect." Chanel said, taking the pizza box out of his hands.

"Yeah, I told you I would have it. You got that for me?" The fiend was desperate for the prime dope he was promised.

"Here's a little teaser," Chanel said, tossing him a small package of dope. "I'll give you the rest after you deliver this. I'll be back in a few minutes," she said, getting back in the car.

The dope fiend stepped away to get his drug fix, which gave Chanel time to put everything needed in place to implement her plan.

About fifteen minutes later, she was ready. "Come on, it's time for you to take this to the building."

"No problem…um…you got some more for me?"

"A lot more, so go 'head and do what you're supposed to do, and I'll be right here waiting. You do remember what you're supposed to say, right?"

"Yeah, yeah…I got you."

Chanel watched as the dope fiend walked away

with the box. She made sure she gave him enough dope so that he would be feeling good, but not so much that he couldn't function and follow directions.

The dope fiend stayed on course, thinking about the hit that would be waiting for him. His mind was so fixated on getting back to the drugs that he hardly paid attention to how much heavier the pizza box now was. He walked up the stairs, and two of the lookout men noticed him coming up. Because he was a regular customer, they let him walk right through the door.

"Man, why the fuck you got that pizza? I know you ain't try'na exchange pizza for drugs! You better get your broke ass on!" one of the crewmembers said, halfway joking.

"Come on. You know I'm good for it. I know you all got to be hungry. My money's a little short, but I got you tomorrow. But take this pizza. It's hot too. I just jacked it from a delivery guy."

"Yo' take that fuckin' pizza! I'm hungry as shit!" one of the other crewmembers barked.

"Me too," another chimed in.

"Give me this damn pizza, and get the fuck outta here!"

"What about my shit?" the dope fiend wanted to know.

"Nigga, I ain't givin' you shit! Come back when you got that green shit called money!" he laughed. "Damn, motherfucker! What type of pizza's up in this bitch? This shit heavy as hell!"

When the crewmember opened the box, his question was answered. He first zoomed in on the note written on the inside:

Arnez told me to tell you hello…

He dropped the box, but he and everybody in the vicinity were fucked. The bomb went off, and the entire building blew up in smoke, leaving no survivors.

When the building went up in flames, Chanel smiled with admiration at her work, and drove off.

*****

"Oh baby, I think that's the best sex we've ever had," Denise purred breathlessly after sliding off from riding Delondo's dick.

"Yeah, that shit was good," he moaned. "You put it on me like you was going for broke."

"You so silly. But you know I felt good," Denise smirked.

"No doubt."

"The other day when I left my phone in your car, did you go through my contacts and check text messages? Tell the truth, I won't get mad."

"Nope, I know you're mine."

"You sound real confidant, especially since you told me you're seeing other women. What I look like being true to you," Denise countered in a flirtatious tone.

"Oh, so you're seeing other men? I take it that's why Arnez was coming out of your apartment the other day."

"Who?" Denise prayed her facial expression matched the calmness of her voice, because on the inside her heart had collapsed to the bottom.

"Arnez, that nigga we saw a few weeks back when we were out to eat."

Denise pretended to be trying to remember who he was.

"When I was coming back to your apartment to give you your phone, I saw him coming out. Is he one of the niggas you fuckin' with?"

"Oh, him! No, I'm not fuckin' with him."

"Then it must be Monica."

"Yeah, but I don't think she's fuckin' with him like that. I think she met him recently."

"You didn't recognize him from the time we were out?"

"No, that's crazy. I had no idea that was the same man."

"He didn't remember you neither?"

"If he did, he didn't mention it. But when I came in, I went straight back to my room. We only saw each other for a few seconds."

"Good. You need to stay away from that nigga, because he's foul. Monica don't need to be fuckin' around with him, but that's on her."

"She didn't seem to be diggin' him, so I doubt he'll be around too much."

"Well, if he is, you'll be at my crib, because I don't want you nowhere near him."

"Baby, you don't have to worry. You're the only man I want near me."

Delondo gripped Denise's ass and pulled her close for a kiss. He had to admit to himself that he was catching real feelings for her. It snuck up on him, and now that he believed she had no dealings with Arnez, he didn't feel the need to fight them. He was willing to give in to his emotions and see what could happen between the two of them.

"You ready to go another round?" Denise asked between kisses.

Right when Delondo was all set to oblige, both his cell phones started going off and they wouldn't stop ringing.

"Yo', what's up?"

"It's been a situation. You need to get over here."

"What type of situation?"

"There was an explosion. The crew is done."

"Done?"

"Yeah, wiped out."

"I'm on my way." Delondo dropped the phone and sat up on the side of the bed and put his head down."

"Baby, what happened?"

Delondo didn't answer for a few seconds because he was in shock. "My crew is dead," he revealed to Denise as if he still didn't believe it himself.

"What…what happened?"

"There was some sort of explosion. I gotta go. Will you be a'ight here until I get back?"

"Of course. Baby, I'm so sorry."

As the news sank in, the only person who kept popping up in Denise's mind was Arnez. He told her Delondo was going down with or without her help, and she had no uncertainty that he was behind whatever went down tonight. Denise wanted to warn Delondo, but she had just denied knowing him and didn't want to appear to be a liar when it seemed they were finally making progress with their relationship.

Damn you, Arnez! You have to be stopped, because there is no way I'm going to let you take out Delondo. And that's that on that! Denise promised herself.

Chapter Fourteen
Decisions

"How does your client plea?" The judge asked.

"Not guilty." Genesis replied sternly, at his arraignment hearing.

"Your Honor, I ask that bail be set for my client," Genesis' attorney requested.

"Your Honor," the prosecutor quickly interjected, "he can't be serious. His client was just apprehended after being on the run for months."

As Genesis' attorney attempted to make a meaningful argument as to why bail should be set for his client, Genesis stared off, halfway listening and halfway recalling the last time he was in front of a judge. He was only eleven years old and that ordeal changed the rest of his life. He had killed his father in an attempt to save his mother but in the end lost both. Genesis spent the majority of his informative years locked up and now as a man the Feds wanted him to spend the rest of his life caged up behind bars. Part of Genesis wanted to blame the system for turning him into a criminal because all he learned when he was in juvenile detention was the only way to survive in the streets was to become a better criminal. Then another part of him wanted to blame his mother and father who brought him into a world of mayhem. Why did he have to be born to a father who was a drug addict, a drunk and a woman beater? And why was he born to a mother who was so weak she let a man beat her with his fist, a pot or anything else he could get his hands on? Why didn't he have a life like some little boys who had a father that played sports with them, or a mother who protected their child from the craziness of the world? Genesis couldn't help but wonder how different his life would be if he did have that life. He had promised himself that one day everything he was deprived of he would someday give it to his own son, but if the prosecution had their way it would never happen. Instead he would just be a statistic, another black man who would die in prison.

"Bail denied!" Those words echoing from the judge's mouth snapped Genesis out of his thoughts.

"Don't worry. We discussed this. With you going on the run, I already told you that more than likely bail would be denied. But I'm working on having the case dismissed. I'll come to see you at the end of the week so we can discuss."

*****

After what seemed like forever and a day, CoCo's attorney had finally made good on his promise to get in front of a judge for a bail hearing. She was praying that she would be tasting freedom soon. She sat with her hands crossed and head halfway titled down. She listened intently as her attorney made an excellent argument as to why bail should be set. CoCo felt what would boost her chances the most was that she had no prior arrest record.

"Bail set for one million dollars…next case."

"Thank you Jesus," CoCo mumbled in a low voice. She had been locked up for months and although she was maintaining her looks physically, as strong as she was, she was beginning to crack mentally.

"So when am I getting out of her?" CoCo wanted to know.

"As soon as bail is posted," her attorney replied.

CoCo looked over her shoulder knowing for sure her sister had to be in the courtroom with a briefcase of money ready to get her the fuck out.

"Umm…where is Chanel? I know she got whatever money you need."

"She wasn't able to make it."

"Did you not tell her my bail hearing was today?"

"Yes, I did inform her but an emergency came up and she wasn't able to make it."

"What's a bigger emergency than me getting the fuck outta here!"

"Lower your voice. I'll call your sister. I'm sure you will be out of here shortly." CoCo slit her eyes at her attorney. She didn't want to go back to prison she wanted to go home. Each day she was spending in jail was draining the life out of her.

*****

"I don't know how much longer I can pull this shit off," Denise confided to Monica.

"Me neither. Pretending to be helping Arnez, you can only fake that shit for so long. He ain't no dummy. Pretty soon, he'll get hip that you're feeding him bullshit."

"He's already starting to put the pressure on me. And I don't know how many more excuses I can come up with as to why I can't set Delondo up for him to be killed by Arnez's people."

"Girl, you playing a dangerous game. You need to come clean to Delondo…now!"

"But he'll hate me."

"But you'll hate yourself if he ends up dead and you could've prevented that shit. I'm telling you, you need to come clean. Because of you helping out Arnez last time, Genesis lost his best friend. Are you willing to lose your man this time around, fuckin' with Arnez's deceitful ass?"

Knock…knock…knock

"I wonder who that is," Denise said as she and Monica both glanced at the door. "I'll get it." Denise walked over to the window and looked out through the blinds. "Speaking of the devil!"

"Aren't you going to invite me in?"

"No! What are you doing here anyway? I thought we agreed that you shouldn't come over here anymore."

"I needed to see you."

"Arnez, you know my cell number. You should've called me and I could've come to you. You don't need to be here. Delondo could pop up and see you here."

"Then I won't stay long."

"You don't need to stay at all!"

"Calm down. Let me come in for a couple of minutes and then I'll leave." Arnez pushed his way in, not waiting for Denise to oblige his request.

Denise slammed the door, infuriated. "What do you want, Arnez?"

"Tomorrow it's going down. Have Delondo meet you here in the early evening around seven o'clock."

"Here? You want to kill Delondo here, at my crib?" Denise pointed her finger down at the floor, completely stunned over the idea.

"Yes. It's an easy place to get him without conjuring up any suspicion."

"It's bad enough that you're making me help you set up my man to be killed, but now you want me to do it at my crib! What the fuck is wrong with you?" Denise noticed Monica in the background making silent gestures for her to calm down.

"Listen, you've been bullshitting me long enough over this. I had damn near all his men wiped out to gain back my territory. But instead of this nigga falling back, he immediately imports another crew to hold shit down. You know how much fuckin' money I'm losing behind that shit? The only way to alleviate this problem and get my projects back is to erase the man who is running the show. That means Delondo has to go. I'm done playing with him, and I'm done playing with you."

"Fine. I'll have Delondo here tomorrow at seven.

But please don't have him killed inside of this apartment."

"Honoring your sentimental pleas for your boyfriend wasn't part of the agreement. Now excuse me, I have other business dealings to handle."

Tonya watched from her car as Arnez came out of Denise and Monica's apartment. She had witnessed what seemed to be a tongue lashing from Denise when he first arrived. That gave Tonya a strong belief that it wasn't Monica who had a personal relationship with Arnez, but instead it was Denise. The nature of their relationship still had her puzzled. Tonya wanted to confront Denise with the little information she had, but knew she didn't have enough ammo for Denise to come clean, especially since lying was second nature to her. Instead, Tonya decided to continue to wait and investigate. She had no doubt that all the pieces to the puzzle would eventually fall into place if she remained patient.

"What are you going to do?" Was the first question out of Monica's mouth when Arnez left.

"I don't know. I mean, I do know, but I don't know how I'm gonna do it, if that makes any sense."

"No, it doesn't," Monica huffed.

Denise didn't need Monica to tell her that, because it didn't make sense to her either. She was starting to feel like she was losing her mind. Nothing seemed logical to her anymore.

"How in the hell did it come to this?" Denise eyes swelled with tears. "I have to tell Delondo the truth, tonight. I can't wait. Arnez is heartless. He's gonna kill him right here. How can someone be so cold?" She sat down on the couch, not able to keep her composure any longer. "This is so bad, Monica," she said and shook her head, as if the magnitude of the situation had finally kicked in.

"I know." Monica sat down next to Denise and wrapped her arm around her shoulder. "But you don't have a choice, you have to tell Delondo."

"You're right." Denise grabbed her cell from off the table. Her fingers were shaking as she retrieved his number from speed dial.

"What's up, baby?" Delondo answered. His smooth voice put Denise at ease for a moment.

"Delondo, I have to see you."

"I wanna see you too. Are you home?"

"Yes."

"Cool. I have to finish some things up and then I'll come get you."

"No, don't come here," she said, worried that Arnez may come back. "I'll meet you at your place."

"Why, when I can just come get you?"

"I'll explain when I get there."

"What's going on? Is everything okay?"

"No, but I want to talk to you in person."

"A'ight. I'll see you at my place in an hour," he said, and they both hung up.

"Denise, I know you scared, but you're doing the right thing. If you want me to, I'll come with you."

"As much as I would love to have you there for support, I need to do this alone. But just be here for me when I get back, because I know I'ma need you."

"I got you." Monica held her close, hoping it would all work out for the best.

Chapter Fifteen
Aftermath

"Baby, I'm sorry I got held up," Delondo said when he opened the door to let Denise in.

"That's okay. I needed the extra time to work up the nerve to tell you what I'm about to say."

Delondo closed the door and eyed Denise strangely. "What, we about to play a game of confessions?"

"I have some confessions to make, but it's absolutely *not* a game."

"You sound serious."

"It is." Denise hadn't even been there for a full five minutes, and she was already getting choked up.

"Denise, are you about to cry?" Delondo pulled her in close and rubbed her back. "Baby, what's wrong? Tell me. Whatever it is, we'll get through it."

"I would tell you to promise me that, but it wouldn't be fair to you."

"Babe, what the fuck could be so bad?" Delondo asked, pulling Denise away so he could look in her eyes for answers. "Tell me, what is it?" he questioned, holding her chin up, with his voice oozing with concern.

"Please don't hate me."

"Yo', you really starting to fuckin' scare me. What is going on?"

Denise took a deep breath. Her nerves were raw, and if she didn't start spitting the truth now, she was afraid she would coward out. "A while ago, I met a guy that I was really feeling."

"Yo' I'm not interested in hearing about some nigga you used to fuck with, unless you telling me you started seeing him again while you been with me," Delondo informed her as the tone of his voice rose.

"No, it's not like that."

"Then what?"

"Ple-e-e-e-ease!" Denise yelled out, but in a pleading voice. "Let me tell you this before I lose my nerve."

Delondo nodded his head, letting Denise know he wouldn't interrupt again.

"So, I was really feeling the guy, and I thought he

was really feeling me too. But come to find out, he had a girl he was checking for on a serious tip. He never told me, and I found out through somebody else. The shit really hurt me. The girl who was now with my ex also had an ex, and he wanted her back just like I wanted my ex back. Are you following me?"

"Yeah, I'm following you," Delondo nodded, but in his mind he was wondering what did any of this shit have to do with him. But since he said he wouldn't interrupt, he continued to listen, waiting for Denise to hurry up with the fuckin' point of the story.

"Somehow, her ex found out about me and where I lived. He came to me with what seemed like an innocent proposition. I wanted my man back, and he wanted his girl back."

"Okay, I got that already!" Delondo snapped.

Denise could tell his patience was wearing thin, so she speeded shit up. "He tricked me into giving him information about the whereabouts of my ex so that he could have him killed."

"So what, the nigga ended up killing your ex? On some what, payback shit because he was fuckin' with his ex girl?"

"That was the plan. I thought he was going to try and win his girl back, not literally eliminate the competition."

"So, is your ex dead?"

"No, somehow the shit got fucked up and two of his friends ended up getting killed instead."

"Damn, that's some foul shit! But what's even fouler is what that nigga did. He used you, and you played right into it. But what am I missing? Why are you telling me about that trife shit you were a co-conspirator in, now?"

"Because the dude that was responsible for it is Arnez."

"Arnez? Arnez!" Delondo jumped up off the couch with his right eye twitching. It was something that happened whenever he got overly excited or extremely angry.

"Yes." Denise put her head down, full of embarrassment.

"The same motherfucker you lied and told me you didn't know? Is Monica even fuckin' with that nigga, or was that a lie too?"

"Yes, it was all a lie. But I was so ashamed about what happened. I didn't want anybody to know that I knew Arnez, and how my stupidity contributed to two people losing their lives. Then, when we saw him at that restaurant and you told me how much he disgusted you, I really felt I should keep it a secret."

"So why the fuck are you telling me now, huh, Denise?"

"Because Arnez is basically blackmailing me."

"Oh, I get it. He threatened to expose your secret

to me in exchange for what? What does he want you to do?"

"Set you up, so he can kill you. He was the one that had that project building blown up."

"I had a feeling that motherfucker had something to do with that shit! How long have you known all this?"

"He came to me that day you saw him leaving my apartment."

"That was weeks ago, and you're only telling me this bullshit now?"

"I know. At that time, he didn't tell me he was going to have your crew killed. All he said was that he needed my help to bring you down, and if I didn't do it, I would lose you anyway once he revealed our past. I've been doing everything to stall for time so he couldn't hurt you. But he came over today and said that I had to get you to my apartment tomorrow so he could get rid of you once and for all."

Delondo was pacing the floor in silence, but his body language was speaking volumes.

"Delondo, say something!"

Without warning, Delondo reached down and grabbed Denise like a ragdoll and slammed her against the wall. Her eyes widened in fear. "I'm not sure if you're as stupid as this story makes you appear, or if you're naïve, or if you're a calculating snake. But whichever one it is, I'm done with you.

And because I'm not positive which category you fall into is the only reason I'ma let you live," Delondo told her calmly. "But I want you to leave and I never want to see your face again. If you catch me in the streets, go in the opposite direction, because next time I may not be so generous with your life."

Denise swallowed hard, trying to hold back the tears that were determined to break free. And she lost the battle as they began streaming down her face. "Delondo, please forgive me. I'm so sorry. I was stupid and I was naïve, but can't you see that I care about you? That's why I told you the truth, because I don't want anything to happen to you. I love…"

Delondo cut Denise off, screaming, "Don't use the word 'love' to describe this madness!" He slammed his fist against the wall, barely missing Denise's face. "You're every hustler's worse nightmare. Now, get out!"

"But Delondo…"

"Now!" He grabbed Denise by her arm, opened the door and threw her out, then slammed the door.

Denise sat on the steps outside his crib and cried for a minimum of fifteen minutes. In her warped mind, she somehow believed that if enough tears flowed for an extended amount of time, Delondo would believe that she was sincere about her love for him and give her another chance.

But for Delondo, it didn't matter if she cried a river. Denise was officially a liability, and in his line of business, that was an automatic veto.

*****

CoCo sat stoned faced across from Chanel. Why has it been two weeks, and I'm still locked the fuck up? Explain that shit to me."
"I'm working on it."
"What the fuck is there to work on? Bail has been set, pay that shit so I can bounce."
"I'm having some difficulty getting the money up."
"Difficulty? What the fuck are you talking about? We got access to more than enough paper to pay that shit."
"I've caught a lot of bad breaks since you've been locked up. One of the stash spots got ran up in, and a lot of money was stolen. Then a new connect I thought I would be doing some business with took the product but didn't give me the cash. And let's not talk about your lawyer fees. I've been taking 'L's' left and right," Chanel explained in a low tone.
"And you're just now telling me this shit, when I finally have a chance to get the fuck out?"
"I didn't want to stress you out."

"Give me a fuckin' break! I've *been* stressed, and I'ma keep being stressed as long as I'm caged up in here. If you so concerned about my stress, get me the fuck out!"

"I told you, I'm working on it."

"Then work harder. Shit, call Quentin. He'll give you the money to get me out."

"I know, but I was trying to get the money myself so we wouldn't owe nobody. I know how you hate that."

"At this point, I don't give a fuck if you have to owe my worse enemy. Get me the fuck outta here! Are we clear?"

"Yes, we're clear. I'll have you out by the end of the week."

"When Friday gets here, I don't want to hear no bullshit ass excuses, Chanel."

"You're not. Don't you think I want you out of this prison too?"

"Is that a question? Because I'm starting to wonder."

"CoCo, of course I want you out. I've been busting my ass tryna make this shit pop off for you. I had no clue all this shit was gonna happen. But it's coming back together, and like I said, you'll be out by the end of the week."

"Then we good. I'll see you Friday."

*****

"So, how are you holding up?" the attorney asked Genesis, who was smoking a Newport and trying to keep his thoughts in perspective.

"Listen, you don't have to pretend we're friends, or even like you give a fuck how I'm doing in here. All I want you to focus on is getting me the fuck out," Genesis made it clear as he took another pull off his cigarette.

"I do care, because Quentin wants you out, so I want you out."

Genesis rubbed the back of his neck and turned away, not in the mood to hear any of that shit, even if his attorney was being sincere. "I hear you. Now, do you have any updates for me?" That was the most tactful way he could think of to let his attorney know to move the fuck on.

"The good news is that your co-defendant hasn't turned on you. She isn't cooperating with the prosecution, which only further hurts their case."

"What do they have?"

"Only a written statement from Mr. Walker. They did find a large quantity of money and drugs in a few of the stash houses, but our argument can be that none of it was yours. None of the properties were in your name. One of the charges is heading a continuing criminal enterprise, but it's going to be almost impossible to prove that, especially since no direct evidence points to you. They had begun a wire tap, but Mr. Walker got killed before any damaging evidence could be recorded."

"Did you find out how they knew I was going to be at the airport in Miami?"

"From what I've gathered, they were tipped off, by whom, I have no idea. But you shouldn't focus on that. Beating this case is what's important. We go before the judge in three weeks to make oral arguments about why the charges against you should be dismissed."

"Is it the same judge from the bail hearing?"

"No, it isn't."

Genesis caught the slight grin on his attorney's face. "I guess that's a good thing."

"It's excellent. Like I said, Quentin wants you out, and I will do everything in my power to make that happen."

Chapter Sixteen
It's Been To Long

"Hello."

"Is this Talisa?"

"Yes, who is this?"

"Genesis asked me to call you."

Talisa put her hand over her chest as if to make sure her heart didn't stop beating. "Genesis! Is he okay?"

"He's fine. He wants to see you."

"Where is he?"

"He's in jail."

Talisa wasn't sure if she should be relieved or crushed that Genesis had been captured. But knowing he was alive and safe was all that mattered. "When can I see him?"

"He has you scheduled for Saturday. Is that too soon?"

"No, I'll be there. Just tell me where to go."

"I'll make the arrangements for you. Will you be leaving out of Philadelphia?"

"No, I'm in New York."

"Which airport is closer to you?"

"JFK."

"I'll call you back in an hour with your flight arrangements."

"Okay, I'll be waiting." Talisa ended her call and looked down at her stomach. "We're going to see your daddy in a couple of days. There's no hiding you now," she smiled, rubbing her now vast belly.

After Talisa's collapse, the doctors kept her in the hospital for a week to monitor her and the baby's health. When it was time to be discharged, she agreed to go back to New York with her father. Talisa really didn't have a choice. Her physical condition had deteriorated to the point that both her and the baby's lives were in jeopardy.

For weeks, her parents made her cut off all communication from the outside world—no phone, no television—nothing. Just rest and eating properly so she could regain her strength. It worked, because gone was the frail frame and tiny baby bump. Talisa had put on weight and had the pregnancy glow that had been lacking for the first few months due to all her stress. She was very reluctant at first, but she now had to admit that coming home to her parents' estate was the best decision she could have made.

"How are you feeling this morning?" her mother asked as she joined Talisa outside by the pool.

"I'm feeling great. And this beautiful weather doesn't hurt."

"You look happy. I haven't seen that since you got here."

"For these last few weeks I haven't had much reason to be happy."

"What's changed?"

"I'm going to see Genesis on Saturday."

"Really? He's finally resurfaced?"

Talisa could hear the disdain in her mother's voice, but refused to allow it to kill her joy. "Yes, and I'll be able to tell him he's going to be a father, although my stomach will tell him for me," she giggled.

"Where is he?" her mother asked, not amused.

"He's in jail."

"Good morning to my two favorite ladies," Talisa's father greeted the women, giving each a kiss on their forehead.

"Good morning, Daddy."

"Good morning Jeffery. Our daughter has wonderful news for us. She's going to see the father of her child in jail this Saturday."

"Is that right?"

"Daddy, please don't try to stop me. Genesis doesn't even know I'm pregnant."

"Well, maybe if he had called you he would have," her mother ridiculed.

"Relax, dear. We don't want to upset Talisa," her father said, patting his wife's leg. "Talisa, you know how I feel about the situation, but I'm not going to try and stop you from seeing this man, Genesis."

"Daddy, he's not 'some man', he's the father of your grandchild."

Talisa's mother rolled her eyes in disapproval.

"You're right, he is."

"That's why, Daddy, if you can help him in any way to get out of jail, I want you to. Please!"

"I can't promise anything, but I'll do what I can."

"You mean that?"

"One thing I've never done is be dishonest with you, Talisa. I don't like or approve of the type of man you've decided to be with, but if I can help him get out of jail so he can be around to raise his child, then I will. I'm not only doing it for you, but also for my grandbaby."

"Thank you, Daddy. You've always been such an amazing man." Talisa started fanning her eyes as the tears crept up. "I'm being extra emotional right now. Blame it on my hormones."

"No need to explain yourself. Now, give me a hug."

Talisa stood up and wrapped her arms around

her dad. No matter what took place in her life, her father's support never dwindled.

"I'm starving. I'm going inside to get me something to eat."

"Okay, dear. We'll see you in a little bit," her father said, warmly.

"You've always spoiled her, and now her life is a complete mess. Never did I imagine I would have a pregnant daughter going to visit her baby's daddy in jail. How did such a cruel joke get played on me?"

"Stop it! We're about to have our first grandchild. There is nothing cruel about that."

"Jeffrey, please! This is a nightmare. Maybe if Talisa didn't have that jailbird as the father lurking in the background, this situation could be doable. But with…" her voice trailed off in frustration.

"We have to make the best of it. The last thing we want to do is alienate her. Then we would lose her and our grandchild. I won't allow that to happen under any circumstances."

"So, you're really going to see what you can do to help him get out of jail?"

"I'm a man of my word. You've never known me to be dishonest, and I'm not about to start with our daughter. If I can help the young man out, then I will. End of story."

*****

Knock…knock…knock

"Who the fuck could be at my door?" Delondo wondered out loud. He reached in the nightstand drawer and took out the forty-five he kept there. Only a few people knew where he rested his head. But with the war he had going on in the streets right now against Arnez, he had to be cautious.

Knock…knock…knock

"Delondo, open up the door. It's me, Tonya."
Delondo kept his gun close just in case his enemy was using Tonya as a decoy to get to him. He looked out of the window and didn't notice anything suspicious, so he let her in. "Why are you here so early in the morning?"
"Why are you answering the door holding a gun?"
"Somebody could've had a gun aimed at your back, making you knock on my door, using you to get at me."
"Yo, you paranoid."
"Call it whatever the fuck you like, but shit is real out here in these streets right now. I'm at war with another nigga, and shit is real ugly."

"Who are you at war with?"

"That snake nigga, Arnez. You know, the one I was telling you about."

"The one you thought the girl you're messing with might be connected to?" Tonya used the opening Delondo gave to pry further, because Denise had become untraceable. After the day she saw her exchanging words with Arnez, she seemed to have disappeared. Tonya had run out of places to look, so she made the decision to come to see her cousin in hopes that he would know what was up. She figured she would have to divulge some information about Denise to get Delondo to fess up to anything he knew, but to her surprise, she caught him at a moment where he was amped and ready to say whatever.

"*Was* messing with. I cut her off!"

"Why, what did you find out?"

"That stupid broad *did* know Arnez?"

"He was messing with her and not the roommate?"

"No, her dumb ass had schemed with that nigga against some ex boyfriend of hers, and ended up getting his friends killed because of petty bullshit. Then, the nigga, Arnez started using her dumb ass again to try to have me set up. I told that silly ho she had to go."

"I suppose she didn't tell you the name of that ex they schemed on."

"I didn't care, so no, I didn't need to fuckin' ask." And neither did Tonya, because she already knew exactly who that ex was. His name was Genesis.

From the time Talisa told her Arnez was responsible for what happened to Deuce, and then Delondo inadvertently mentioning his suspicions that either his girl or her roommate had dealings with a cat named Arnez, Tonya knew Denise was involved in some foul shit. To what extent had now been revealed and any doubts were now squashed. Not only was Denise the sloppy slut she always pegged her to be, but in Tonya's mind she was also responsible for Deuce's murder, and it was time for her to pay up.

Chapter Seventeen
Pain & Torture

When Talisa arrived at the Federal Prison in Georgia, she was nervous and anxious. She hadn't seen Genesis in months, but to her it felt like years. She sat patiently, waiting for him to come out. When she caught the profile of Genesis' face as he was being escorted in, all the longing and aching from missing him ripped through her body. She believed that seeing him for the first time in so long would ease her heartache, but it seemed to make her feel worse. Here was the man that she loved so much and hadn't stopped dreaming about since the day he left, and he was so close, but yet so far away. She wanted to hold him, touch his skin, feel his lips against hers, but none of that was possible. It was pure torture.

"Talisa, baby, thank you for coming." His voice still soothed her mind like no other.

"Of course I came. I've been begging for this day to happen for so long. The only part I hate is seeing you under these circumstances. But at least I've finally gotten to see you."

"Do you forgive me?"

"Forgive you for what? You haven't done anything."

"For leaving you."

"I know why you had to do that. I understand, and you don't have to apologize to me for it. All I want us to do is focus on getting you out of here."

"My attorney's working on that. I have a hearing coming up in a few weeks."

"When? I want to be there."

"I'll make sure someone gets in touch with you with all of the information."

"Promise me you'll do that. We're in this together, all three of us."

"Three?"

Talisa stood up and turned to the side and held her stomach. She watched as Genesis' mouth dropped and his eyes watered up.

"You're carrying my baby…my child!" his strong voice cracked.

"Yes, I'm carrying your baby. I love you so much."

"I love you too. Did you know you were pregnant before I left?"

"Yes. I wanted to surprise you with the news, then Deuce got killed, and then this whole incident."

"You know I would've never left you if I knew you were pregnant. I'm so sorry. I know how hard these last few months must've been for you."

"Baby, it's okay. Dealing with this made me realize that I'm a lot stronger than I thought I was."

"Where are you staying now?"

"At my parents' place in New York."

"I know they must feel some type of way that the father of your child is behind bars," Genesis said, putting his head down. "I'm supposed to be there for you and our child, not locked the fuck up."

"And you will be. There is no doubt in my mind. But baby, listen, I know my visitation is about to be up, and I have to tell you something before I leave."

"What is it?"

"I know who's responsible for what happened to Deuce."

Genesis gripped the phone tightly and his jaw clenched. "Who?"

"Arnez. He called me the day it happened. He meant to get you."

"Why didn't you tell me?"

"Because you went to such a dark place after

what happened. It was like I couldn't even reach you. And then when I was going to tell you, you left."

"So, Arnez knows that you know. Has he been bothering you?"

"He came by a month or so ago and tried to scare me."

"Did he hurt you? Don't lie!"

"No. He thinks the baby might be his. That's the only reason why he didn't."

"Is there a chance that it could be?"

"No! Absolutely not! But I didn't tell him that because you know how crazy he is, and I didn't want to give him any reason to harm me or our baby. But I haven't been staying at the condo since I had that run-in with him."

"Good. Keep it that way, because if he did anything to you or our baby…" Genesis' voice trailed off and then went silent, but Talisa could tell by the fire in his eyes what his mind was thinking.

Talisa put her hand against the glass that was separating them. "Baby, don't worry. I'm going to make sure me and our baby remain safe."

"You better, because that's all I'm living for right now," Genesis' said, putting his hand up against Talisa's from the other side of the glass.

*****

Tonya had been plotting, waiting, and plotting some more ever since she left Delondo's crib and got confirmation about Denise. After almost a week without making any progress, her fortitude had finally paid off and Denise came out of hiding. Tonya watched as she pulled up in her car during the middle of the night. *I wonder who this heffa's been hiding from? Probably Arnez. But then again, she's so trifling it could be any fuckin' body*, Tonya thought to herself. She tapped her fingers on the steering wheel as Denise got out of her car. She seemed to be checking all around before going inside her apartment. Although Tonya was parked a good distance away, she slid down in her seat to make sure Denise didn't catch a glimpse of her face.

Tonya eyed her watch, and when ten minutes had passed, she decided to make her move.

Knock…knock…knock

"Who could be at the door this time of night?" Monica looked at Denise and asked.

"Oh shit! Do you think it could be Arnez?" Denise questioned nervously. "I mean, damn, I didn't see nothing suspicious when I drove up and I haven't been here for awhile, so how would that motherfucker know I'm back?"

"Shh!" Monica put her finger over her mouth. She then went to the peephole. "It's Tonya," Monica said, looking all types of confused.

"What the hell does she want?" Denise asked with a frown on her face.

Knock...knock...knock

"Tonya, what are you doing here, this time of night?" Monica asked, with the door halfway open.

"Monica, I'm so glad you're up. I was worried about you."

"Worried about me? Why?"

"Can I come in? I really don't want to talk out here."

Monica hesitated for a second, but then let Tonya come inside. "So, what's up, Tonya? What got you so concerned that you're making after-hour house calls?"

Tonya could hear the annoyance in Monica's voice, but she could give a flying fuck. She had an agenda that would be followed through to the fullest.

"Yeah, what do you want?" Denise chimed in, smacking her lips.

It took all of Tonya's strength not to jump over the couch and stomp Denise, but she knew

Monica would jump in and help her, which would defeat the purpose. "I was at this lounge with my girlfriend a little while ago, and she started talking to me about this nigga she fuck with."

"And?" Denise grunted with her hand on her hip.

"Although I don't care what happens to you, Denise," she said before turning her attention towards Monica, "He told her how this foul ass bitch he knows went missing, and that if she didn't show up soon, he was going to send her a message by killing her roommate."

Tonya watched as the color drained from Monica's face. She then turned towards Denise, who had also lost all the pigmentation from her skin.

"What makes you think that has anything to do with us?" Monica was trying to remain calm, as if she didn't know what Tonya was talking about.

"My girlfriend doesn't have any idea that I'm cool with you, so she mentioned both of your names."

"She must be talking about another Monica and Denise. Better yet, Tonya, you probably just came over here trying to start some bullshit between me and Monica. See, Monica, you shoulda never let this bitter bitch in here."

"Monica, do you know a dude named Arnez? Because that's the nigga she said told her."

"Yo', I knew that motherfucker was crazy! I shoulda never got in the middle of this bullshit!" Monica said nervously.

"I take it then that you all do know this Arnez. Well, I'll be damned! What have you done now, Denise, that you put Monica's life in danger?"

"I don't know what the fuck you talking about. Monica, don't listen to her. She's just running off at the mouth and don't know what the fuck she's talking about."

"Just stop, Denise! This shit has gone too far. Maybe we need to go to the police. I mean, I don't see no other way out of this bullshit. I ain't tryna die fuckin' around with you and Arnez!" Monica screamed as she made her way past Tonya, going towards Denise.

"Monica, calm down. Ain't no need for us to go to the police yet."

"Denise, you know that nigga is straight up crazy! If we would've went to the police months ago, we wouldn't be in this predicament right now. If we don't turn Arnez in, we both gon' end up dead, and that's real talk right there."

"What happened months ago?" Tonya questioned, as if she was clueless.

"None of your damn business! You've delivered your little message, now get the fuck out!" Denise spit.

"I was hoping that Denise had kept you in

the dark about what she did, Monica. But unfortunately for you, that isn't the case." Both women turned and looked at Tonya.

"Tonya, why are you talking in riddles?"

"Denise, do you ever shut the fuck up and listen? I'm not talking in riddles. In fact, what I'm saying makes perfect sense, doesn't it, Monica?"

"How long have you known?"

"Monica, she doesn't know anything. She came over here trying to trip us up. We don't have to tell her nothing!"

"I don't need for you to tell me nothing, you low life bitch! Because of your deceitful dumb ass, Deuce is dead! You might as well have pulled that trigger yourself!"

"Fuck you, Tonya! I never meant for Deuce to die, or anybody else. Arnez is the one who is responsible, not me! Now, get the fuck out!" Denise barked.

"I'm not going anywhere until I'm done here." Tonya reached in her purse and brandished the gun she stole from Delondo's apartment.

"Tonya, that shit ain't funny. You've made your point. I should've come clean with you from the jump, but just like you were my friend, so was Denise, and she was truly remorseful about what happened."

"We ain't friends. You made your choice when you kept riding with that heffa," Tonya said, pointing her finger at Denise. "That bitch ain't shit, but you stayed fuckin' with her snake ass. Now, she's about to cost you your life."

"Fuck that!" Denise belted as she grabbed the glass vase off the table and threw it towards Tonya, making her lose her balance and fall back.

During the commotion, Monica reached for the cordless phone and dialed 911 as the women tried to make a dash towards one of the bedrooms to lock themselves in.

"What's the emergency?" Monica heard the operator ask, but before she could respond, a bullet exploded through her shoulder. The excruciating pain made her drop the phone.

"You crazy bitch!" Denise cried out, tugging at Monica's other arm to pull her down the hallway into the bedroom. But between the trigger-happy Tonya and the speed of the bullets, the women didn't stand a chance.

"Awww!" Monica howled as the next bullet ripped through her back, causing her to fall face first to the floor, and bringing Denise down with her.

Denise looked up, and staring down at her was the barrel of the gun. "Don't do this, Tonya! I swear, it wasn't my fault. It was Arnez. He's the one that did this!" Denise pleaded.

"Best believe Arnez will get his too," Tonya said, right before emptying her gun in Denise.

Tonya stood over Monica and Denise for a few

minutes, relishing in the damage she'd done. She found pleasure and satisfaction in knowing that she had begun the process of getting retribution for what was done to Deuce.

"Drop the gun and put your hands up!" a police officer shouted after kicking the front door open. But Tonya didn't move. "Drop the gun and put your hands up!" the officer repeated.

A suicide mission wasn't part of Tonya's original plan, but she was also well aware that shit could quickly go horribly wrong. And one thing was for certain; she had no intentions of doing life for taking out two birds as worthless as Monica and Denise. That simply wasn't even in the cards.

Tonya had no qualms about meeting her demise, because as far as she was concerned, she had now honored Deuce's death, and accomplishing that had been her only motivation for living all these months. She wished she had the opportunity to watch Arnez die, but she had faith that either Genesis or Delondo would see to that.

She slowly turned around, and there were now several officers on the scene. The police sirens were blaring and guns were drawn. But instead of dropping her weapon like she was ordered to do, Tonya pointed it directly at the officer, with her finger firmly on the trigger. There were no bullets left in the gun, but of course the police officer didn't know that, and that's what Tonya counted on.

The police officer didn't give another warning. Instead, they riddled her body with bullets, and the gunshots didn't come to a halt until her bloody body was lying on top of her former friends.

Chapter Eighteen
Game On

"God is good!" CoCo repeated over and over again as she walked out of prison, hoping to never return. "Where's Chanel?" was the first question to her attorney.

"She sent me to pick you up. I thought it would be better this way."

"*You* thought it would be better? Why is that?"

"With the Feds already having their eyes on you, we don't want to bring any unnecessary heat to your sister too."

"I would've thought by now that if the Feds were gon' bring it to Chanel, it would've been brought."

"You never know with them, and whenever

possible, it's better to be cautious."

"Fine. I'll roll with that, but umm, wherever we're about to go, is my sister there waiting for me?"

"Chanel will be here in a few days. She had to tend to some business in Philadelphia."

"I'm confused. What business was so important that she couldn't be here for her sister when she got out of jail? But that's cool."

CoCo sat in the back of the Town Car, fuming. She couldn't fathom what had Chanel so preoccupied that she wouldn't be there upon her release. She thought about Arnez, and whether Chanel was sprung out and in Philly chasing the dick, but she felt that wasn't Chanel's style. Then CoCo remembered the last conversation they had and how Chanel went on about the financial hit the business took. CoCo decided it had to be about business, because money could be the only reason her sister would bail on her.

"So you know, Mr. Taylor's attorney has a hearing scheduled in a few weeks to get the charges dismissed against his client."

"What are the chances that could happen?"

"Honestly, it could go either way. I've stated from day one that the prosecution's case is very weak. But a lot of times with hearings of that nature, it depends on the judge."

"Why haven't you had the same hearing for me?

I've been locked up way longer than Genesis."

"I was waiting to see what happened with his case. I wasn't sure once Mr. Taylor was apprehended if he would turn against you and be a witness for the prosecution."

"I told you that would never happen."

"Let's just say that I didn't have as much confidence in him as you did."

"Now you know he's not a snitch. So, what's the holdup?"

"It's better for us to wait and see how his hearing goes. He does have an exceptional attorney who might be able to get the charges dropped, or he may not. Whichever way it goes will give us a strong indication of what will happen at our hearing. But of course, if his attorney is able to get the charges dismissed, more than likely the prosecution won't pursue the case against you."

"I see."

CoCo's mind wandered off as she reflected on the last time she saw Genesis. After all these months, nothing had changed. She was still very much in love with him. One of her biggest regrets was never telling him that. But she vowed to herself that if they were able to beat this case, she wouldn't let another day pass without revealing her true feelings to him.

"We're here," CoCo heard her attorney say, interrupting her thoughts.

"Oh, you play too much! The Red Roof! Is this some sort of joke?" CoCo glanced out of the window, then back at her attorney.

"I know it's not up to your normal standards."

"Do you even know what my normal standards are? This shit cannot be happening to me. I've had people in my crew that been locked up for less than a week, but on the strength of them being locked up in a cage for however long, when they get out, it's Hollywood treatment, at least for the first couple of days. Now, I am the Boss Bitch, and I'm greeted to the fuckin' Red Roof Inn! Get the fuck outta here!"

"CoCo, I understand your frustration, but I believe Chanel explained to you the financial difficulties she's experiencing right now."

"Give me your phone."

"Excuse me?"

"Mr. Katz, give me your fuckin' phone... now!" CoCo demanded, practically reaching in his suit jacket and taking it from him.

He handed CoCo his phone and assumed she was calling her sister.

"Hello."

"Quentin, it's CoCo."

"How's my baby girl? Where are you calling me from?"

"My attorney's cell phone. Quentin, I got released from jail today, and guess where these motherfuckers got me staying at? The Red motherfuckin' Roof! What type of shit is this? And Chanel's not even here!"

"What you need, baby?"

"I need for you to come here. I have no money, no nothing."

"You in Atlanta, right?"

"Yes."

"I'll have one of my people come and take care of you. Whatever you need, it's not a problem."

"I need for you to come. I don't want to see a stranger. I've been locked up with strangers for months. I want to be around someone that I know, a friend, somebody who actually gives a fuck about me."

"Say no more. I'll be on the next flight out."

"Okay, I'm at the Red Roof on Virginia Avenue in Decatur."

"Don't get comfortable, I'm coming to get you."

"Thank you." CoCo ended the call and turned to her attorney and said, "Real recognize real, and some fake ass shit is going on," she remarked, then tossed the cell back at him.

*****

"So, what's our next move?" Chanel sat across

from Arnez at their regular spot, Lacroix, at the Rittenhouse, waiting for him to give her some sort of direction. Shit had seemed to be going so lovely, but now it was quickly turning to shambles.

"Finding out what happened to Denise has taken things in a much more complex direction."

"I told you not to fuck with that silly broad. How different shit would be if you had only listened to me."

"Chanel, cut it. This is not the time for your self-righteous riot act."

"I'm not being self-righteous, I'm simply stating the facts. And the fact is, because you chose to try and negotiate a deal with an empty, weak-minded broad, our whole cover has been blown. Delondo knows you're behind his crew getting killed, and that he's next. He now keeps himself surrounded by so much protection that it's going to be damn near impossible for us to get to him."

"You don't think I know that? Hell, if Denise wasn't dead already, I would kill her myself. The situation with her has put us in a vulnerable position, but it can be handled. We have to find another way to infiltrate Delondo's operation."

"And how do we do that?"

"I'm not sure yet. But we have to come up with something soon, because I'm sure as we speak, Delondo is contriving his own plan to eliminate me. Speaking of eliminating, have you made any progress on our other problem?"

"I assume you're speaking about Genesis' sister."

"Yes, unless there is another problem you're working on that I'm unaware of."

"No, and no. I haven't been able to locate her. But she'll resurface. Plus, Genesis is locked up. She wouldn't be of any benefit to us right now."

"True, but it's always good to have one up on our enemy. So, find her, and when you do, keep a very close tab."

"Will do, but we need to be leaving. I have to catch an early flight tomorrow."

"Where are you going?"

"Remember, I told you CoCo got out on bail."

"Oh yes. I've had so much other shit on my mind, I forgot."

"Robert said she was furious that I wasn't there and that I had her staying at the Red Roof."

"You put CoCo in the Red Roof? Why in the fuck would you do that?"

"Because I told her weeks ago that the reason I couldn't get her out on bail right then was because our finances were fucked up. I'm trying to stay true to that story. If I go from telling her that our cash is dried up to putting her in a suite at the Four Seasons, what type of sense would that make?"

"I hear you, but the last thing we want is to get CoCo riled up. Don't forget, we need her. And the way shit is going on our end, that Quentin connect is more crucial than ever. Yeah, get on that flight and smooth shit over with your sister. I don't give a fuck what you gotta do," Arnez ordered before leaving a hundred-dollar tip on the table. He continued lecturing Chanel as they walked out of the restaurant, following behind his bodyguard.

"Damn! When we came inside it was clear skies, and now it's pouring rain," Arnez remarked as he looked for the car.

"Where did we park?" Chanel tried to remember.

"Don't worry about it, boss. You and Chanel can wait inside. I'll pull the car up here to the front."

"Good looking out," Arnez said, before diverting back to the initial conversation he was having with Chanel. "When you see your sister, put her in the best hotel, take her shopping, to the spa, have her completely pampered, and let her know it's all on me. You understand?"

"Arnez, I got this. I know how to handle CoCo. Relax and…"

Before Chanel could finish her sentence, there was a crackling sound and a *pop-pop-pop-pop*, then a noise as if a dumpster had dropped, followed by a huge ball of flames exploding, lightening up the sky, which had her and Arnez in a daze.

Arnez felt his phone vibrating and fidgeted in his pants pocket to retrieve it, "Hello!" he answered in a shaky voice.

"You wanna blow up buildings, take out my

crew? That car explosion was only a little treat to make it clear that I will be coming for you, one motherfucker at a time."

"Who was that?" Chanel could see the disdain on Arnez's face.

"Fuck! I knew Delondo would strike back, but not like this, not so soon." Arnez stood there shaking his head, knowing the game was officially on.

Chapter Nineteen
New Beginning

"Quentin, thank you so much for coming." CoCo put her arms around Quentin and held him tightly. She knew with him it was all love, and that was something she hadn't felt in a very long time.

"I told you I would be here. You're like my daughter. I would never let you down."

"At least I know one person won't," CoCo groaned.

"Talk to me. What's on your mind?"

"I don't know what's going on with Chanel. She hardly came to see me when I was locked up. I know this might sound crazy, but I felt like she wanted me to stay locked up. And when I do get out, she ain't nowhere around, and she put me in this piece of shit of a motel. The Chanel I knew would never play me out like this."

"Has she given you any sort of explanation?"

"She said shit's been crazy for her, tryna maintain the business with me being locked up, and that she had a couple of bad dealings and lost a lot of money, and that basically, we're broke."

"Broke?"

"Yeah, said the Feds took a lot of it, then we got robbed, and the ridiculous lawyer fees. I mean I know shit can happen, but damn, I can't help but think Arnez is the blame for a lot of her changes."

"What do you mean by that?"

"She hasn't admitted it, but I believe her relationship with Arnez has turned personal. I think they fuckin'."

"Are you sure?"

"I mean, I've been locked up, so it ain't like I caught them in the act, but she told me the reason she hasn't been in Atlanta was because she was in Philly handling some business with Arnez. And she referred to them as *'we'* like they're a couple and shit. When I called her on it, she tried to backtrack. I straight out asked her were they fuckin' and she denied it, but I know my sister, and she was lying."

"I see." Quentin sat on the bed, nodding his head. "Do you believe Chanel is plotting against you?"

"No, nothing like that. I think she might have her nose so far up Arnez's ass that she ain't focused on doing what's best for me, and what's best for us on a business tip. Love, or whatever the fuck is going on, got her slippin'. She ain't concentrating on the most important thing, which is our finances. Ain't no way we're supposed to be broke, and I damn sure shouldn't have to stay in the Red Roof. I've grinded for too many years to get out of jail and come home to this!"

"Don't worry about that, it's already been taken care of. Get your stuff together so we can go."

"Stuff? Please! I ain't got shit! I need new everything."

Knock…knock…knock

"CoCo, are you there? It's me, Chanel."

CoCo glanced at Quentin and then at the door with shock. "Chanel, I wasn't expecting to see you," CoCo said, opening the door.

"Girl, you know I was coming. I missed you! I'm so happy you're out. Give me a hug." The two sisters embraced tightly. "Hey, Quentin, what are you doing here?"

"Hello, Chanel. How are you?"

"Better now that my sister is out. CoCo, I'm so sorry I couldn't be here when you first came out and for putting you up in this hotel room. Money is so tight right now, but Arnez felt so horrible when I told him about our circumstances that he gave me all the money I needed to make sure you're able to maintain like the Queen-pin you are. You ready to leave this dump so I can take you to your new accommodations?" Chanel smiled.

"Chanel, you had me worried for a minute, but I'm glad you didn't let me down, and Arnez stepped up too. I was so stressed the fuck out, I called Quentin to come save the day."

"You know I don't ever mind coming through for you. But Chanel, that was very considerate of Arnez to help you and CoCo out like that."

"Well, you know we did a lot of business in the past with Arnez, and he also thinks very highly of CoCo. He was more than happy to do whatever he could for her."

"But CoCo, my condo in Buckhead is still available to you if you want to use it."

"That's very generous of you Quentin, but CoCo, I hooked you up in the Empire Suite at the new St. Regis Atlanta. Wait 'til you see the room. It's more like a mini-mansion. It's over 2,800 square-feet of pure luxury." Chanel was talking her sister's language as her eyes widened.

"Would you mind, Quentin? You came all this way, and you know I appreciate the condo, but I want to just relax and be waited on. And there is no better place to do that than a five star hotel!"

"I completely understand, and I don't blame you. It was worth coming, if only to see your face," he said, kissing CoCo on the forehead.

"But you don't have to leave."

"I'm not. I have some business to handle here. I'm also going to see Genesis."

"I wish I could go. Please give Genesis my best, and tell him that we will beat this together."

"I will. Call me tomorrow. We can have dinner."

"I will. And Quentin, thanks again for being you, and coming through for me."

"Always good to see you Chanel. I know the two of you have a lot of catching up to do. Enjoy yourselves."

CoCo smiled and waved goodbye to Quentin. She was ecstatic to be out of jail and around her sister. But her heart ached knowing that Genesis was still locked up and being deprived of the simple things that are so easily taken for granted when you're free.

*****

Genesis' mind was flooded with so much information that he felt he was about to fly into a rage, and it all centered around one person—Arnez. Out of all the different scenarios that played in his head surrounding Deuce's death, never did he believe the hit was actually meant for him. Genesis now knew that it was he who was supposed to be six feet under, not his best friend, and it was all because of Arnez's sick obsession with Talisa and his hatred for him. That was eating Genesis up inside.

Then, Genesis reflected on Talisa and how she was carrying his child. He was finally bringing life into this world. He prayed with everything inside of him that he would get out of this cage so he would have the opportunity to not only be a father, but be so much better than the one he had. That was the dream he prayed would be fulfilled as he closed his eyes.

*****

CoCo stood in the center of the suite, taking every detail in. "This is the type of shit I'm talking 'bout right here!" she spread her arms out and yelled. Being surrounded by gloom and doom for the last few months almost made her forget fine living, but entering the open and airy Empire Suite quickly refreshed her memory.

It had a full kitchen and elegant dining area, a piano and fireplace. It was surrounded by

French doors and several small Juliette balconies. Throughout the suite, elegant crown molding, original artwork, and architectural drawings, handcrafted chandeliers and ebony furnishings melded with soothing hues of cream, taupe and mineral green, along with sprays of fresh flowers and the floor-to-ceiling windows that made it even more inviting.

"I knew you would like it!" Chanel announced proudly.

"Of course you did. We're twins, and you know my style. Now, where is my bedroom?" CoCo drifted off, passing the Techno-Gym equipped exercise room on the way. "I can't wait to have a hot bubble bath and soak in this tub," she said, twirling around in the white marble bathroom. "I'm going to have me a bottle of champagne, eat a big juicy steak, watch a movie on the LCD, and pretend the months I spent in jail never happened."

"Sounds good to me. I'ma take the other bedroom, which, by the way, is just as nice." Chanel winked her eye.

"Everything in this motherfucker is nice, so I'm not surprised."

"Do you want to go down to the Remede Spa today, or you wanna wait and maybe do some shopping? Whatever you like."

"Girl, I want to do it all! First, let's hit the spa so I can be pampered. Then, I want to get my hair did.

Believe it or not, I'm digging this short haircut, especially with this hot weather. I want to get it trimmed up nice and put some jet on this black."

"You know what? This is the first time we've never had our hair alike, so I'ma follow your lead. This weave is coming out, and we gon' be rockin' the same haircut, 'cause the shit is fly!"

"That's right, baby. Let's get our hair done, and after that, I want to tear the mall up. Gucci, Chanel and Prada, here I come!"

*****

When Delondo first came in the house, he proceeded with his regular routine of turning the TV on to ESPN, getting a beer out of the refrigerator, and sitting down in his mahogany swirl leather wrapped chair, scanning through his mail. He opened up a few bills, read over some paperwork regarding one of the properties he owned, tossed aside some junk mail, but his heart almost stopped when he came across an envelope addressed to him from his now deceased cousin, Tonya. At first he thought it was some sort of sick joke, but he recognized the handwriting as being hers. He tore open the envelope and unfolded the letter.

Dear Delondo:

If you're reading this letter, it must mean that shit didn't fall in place exactly the way that I wanted, but it was worth it. I never really discussed it with you, but after Deuce got killed, I pretty much gave up on having a reason to live. The only thing that kept me going was that I wanted to know who was responsible for his death and make sure there was payback. Unknowingly, you helped me accomplish part of that, and on everything that I loved, I hope you'll finish what I started.

When that snake, Denise told you about her conspiring with Arnez, what she didn't tell you was the players involved. Genesis was the ex, and "my" Deuce was his best friend that got killed in his place. When I found that out, I had no choice but to take her out of this world. And Monica had to go too, because at one time I considered her a friend, and instead of her coming to me about what Denise had done, she kept me in the dark. Both of those bitches had to die!

I wanted you to hear it from me why I did what I did, and I also want you to make sure that Arnez pays with his life. He doesn't deserve to live.

Love
Tonya

Delondo put the letter down on the table. He wished that Tonya would've opened up to him about what was going on. Maybe she would still be alive. But then, Delondo had to accept that Tonya didn't want to live anymore. *I couldn't save you, Tonya, but I will honor your last request. Arnez is a dead man.*

Chapter Twenty
Taste Of Freedom

Genesis turned around and saw Talisa walk in the courtroom. She never looked more beautiful to him. Her hair was pulled away from her face in a loose ponytail. The pregnancy glow was in full effect, making her skin appear luminous. The white embroidered, strapless maxi dress made her seem angelic to him.

"I love you," Talisa mouthed before taking her seat on the bench.

"I love you too," Genesis mouthed back and turned around to face his attorney. "What's it looking like?"

"Very good," his attorney replied, placing his documents in a neat pile. He was calm and relaxed, which put Genesis at ease. "I was able to get the judge I wanted, so you should be walking out of that prison a free man today," he whispered in Genesis' ear.

Genesis stared back at Talisa again and gave her a quick smile. The thought of him being able to hold Talisa and to feel her stomach that had his seed growing inside sent calmness through his body. Then, seeing and hearing the confidence in his attorney's voice gave him the belief that all would go in his favor, and he would make it home to his family.

"All rise! Honorable Judge Mantineo will be presiding."

"What the hell is going on?" Genesis' attorney mumbled under his breath.

"What's wrong?" His attorney's body language had completely changed. No longer was he calm and cool. Genesis saw a coat of perspiration appearing on his face.

"This isn't the judge we were supposed to argue our case in front of."

"So, what are you saying?"

"There is a very good chance we might get screwed."

Genesis fell back in his chair and put his head down.

Talisa watched as Genesis' once optimistic facial expression turned to gloom, and she wondered why. She wanted to get his attention, but it seemed like he was forcing himself not to look in her direction.

As the hearing began, Talisa's hands started to get sweaty from her nerves getting the best of her. She wanted Genesis to come home and be with her again. The idea of her having and raising the baby alone without him was something she couldn't fathom. She needed him, and so did their child.

The hearing seemed to go on forever as the prosecution and Genesis' attorney went back and forth. The prosecutor was relentless in his determination to make the charges stick, and the opposing attorney came right back just as hard, if not harder.

When both finished arguing their positions, Talisa felt that honestly, it could go either way. The prosecution's evidence was extremely weak, but his fortitude was compelling. It was now in the hands of the judge.

*****

CoCo and Chanel were chilling at the 40,000 square-foot pool piazza, each drinking a mango mojito. They were surrounded by a glowing fireplace, Jacuzzi, and a poolside bar. As the women lounged by the pool, men of all races, ages and economic status couldn't help but fawn over the black beauties. In their matching silk teal, Brazilian low-rise bikini's and newly, perfectly cropped haircuts, you couldn't tell if they were there for a paid photo shoot, or just some bad ass bitches getting their relaxation on.

"I needed this," Chanel said, sipping on her drink. She expected CoCo to co-sign on her comment, but all she got was dead air. "Umm, CoCo, did you hear what I said?"

"Girl, I'm out of it. Repeat that."

"We're damn near close to heaven right now and you're zoning out. What got your mind someplace else?"

"Genesis. His hearing is going on today."

"What hearing?"

"His lawyer filed a motion trying to get the charges against him dropped for insufficient evidence. I'm so worried."

"Don't. There's nothing you can do about it."

"I know, but I want him out of jail. I hate that he's locked up."

"I see your feelings for dude ain't changed."

"Nope. Honestly, I think they're stronger now than they were before."

"I understand how you feel about Genesis, but right now, I think you should concentrate on *your* case. You're out right now, and we damn sure tryna stop you from having to go back."

"My attorney said that if Genesis' attorney can get his case dismissed, more than likely the prosecution won't pursue their case against me. But again, that's a big if. I'm hoping it will happen, because I'm ready to get back in the game and start making some money. Arnez ain't gonna foot this lifestyle for me forever."

"If shit do work out and you're able to beat this shit, I know you're ready to start grinding again. But the Feds will be watching every move you make. It might be best if you fall back for a while."

"Fall back and do what? I can't get no nine-to-five. Hustling is all I know. And ain't no regular job gon' allow me to lounge like this."

"What if there was another way?"

"Another way to what?"

"Retire from the game, but still be able to afford to live like this."

"Girl, please! We ain't talking 'bout a fantasy world, we're talking real life."

"So am I. Hear me out for a second. What if you put Arnez on to all your connects, and he hits you off with a percentage of what he made? Kinda like a broker's fee."

"Arnez already has his own connects."

"True, but he ain't getting the type of volume and price cut you get from Quentin. With that sort of rate and volume, he would completely dominate

Philly and all the other areas we run. I mean after you got locked up, I realized how real shit is out here. I don't want to take another chance that some shit like this could happen to either one of us again."

"I feel you on that, but to completely get out of the game and depend on a man to spoon feed me my money, that shit ain't really me. How do I know Arnez ain't gon' change his mind and be like he don't want to hit me off with a percentage anymore?"

"Arnez wouldn't do that to you. But even if he tried, Quentin would cut him off."

"I wouldn't want to put Quentin in the middle of that. That's crossing the line of putting too much personal shit with business."

"I feel you, but we've known Arnez for a long time. I'ma hundred and fifty percent sure he wouldn't cross you. It's a win-win situation for everybody. We would no longer have to take the risk that comes with the everyday hustle, but still receive all the benefits the game provides."

"It sounds good, but I don't know, Chanel."

"You don't have to decide now. All I ask is that you think about it. Shit, I would love to retire young, so we can relax by the pool, looking sexy as fuck and not having a financial care in the world."

CoCo lowered her sunglasses and smiled at Chanel. "Yeah, I can't front, that shit do sound good as a motherfucker."

The sisters' both laughed and clinked their drinking glasses together.

Chapter Twenty One
Where We Stand

"How was your trip?" Arnez was anxious to find out if he would see a return on his investment, or whether it was a bust.

"I think it was productive."

"Does that mean you're back in your sister's good graces?"

"Yes indeed. She's a big fan of yours too. All that shopping and pampering paid off."

"To the point that she's willing to turn over her business to me?"

"I believe so. I made a very convincing argument."

"You better be right, for your sister's sake."

"Like I told you before, I can handle CoCo. I'm

trying to deal with her in a diplomatic way, and if that doesn't work, we'll go the other route. If my dear sister has to meet her demise, then I'll be the one to take over, and I have no doubt that Quentin will continue to do business directly with me. And Quentin doing business with me is him doing business directly with you."

"You're so fuckin' sexy when you talk business," Arnez said, reaching his arm around Chanel's waist and pulling her against the table. "And did I tell you how unbelievably gorgeous you look with your hair cut like that? My dick has been hard since you walked through the door."

"Did I tell you how wet you've gotten my pussy right now?"

"No, but let me see if you're telling me the truth," Arnez said, lifting Chanel's leg up as he glided his hand up her thigh.

"Ahh!" she moaned as he slid her panties to the side and began finger fucking her.

"You were telling me the truth. This pussy is so wet." Arnez cupped Chanel's ass and sat her on top of the table. He unbuckled his belt and pulled down his slacks, ready for his dick to get swallowed in her warm juices.

"We really do make the perfect team. We're two of a kind," Chanel whispered in Arnez's ear as he filled up her insides.

"I know. Why else do you think I keep you

around?" Arnez replied as he bit down on Chanel's neck, as if ready to suck all the life out of her.

*****

CoCo had been doing nonstop shopping since being out on bail, and today wasn't going to be any different. She was playing catch-up for all the months she was deprived of her favorite past-time.

CoCo didn't want to admit it, but she was also scared that this might be her last time to enjoy her freedom. There was a very good chance she would be doing an extremely long bid in a women's federal prison. If that happened, she wanted to enjoy this time, because she would never get to do so again.

Knock…knock…knock

"Who could that be?" CoCo wondered out loud. "Oh, it's probably the cleaning lady. Good! While I'm out lacing myself with some new clothes, they can freshen the place up," she continued out loud as she went to open the door."

"Long time, stranger!"

"Genesis! I can't believe it's you!" CoCo wrapped

her arms so tightly around his neck she almost made him fall over. "I missed you so much! When did you get out?"

"I missed you too," he said, giving CoCo a kiss on the cheek. She was tempted to grab his face and put her tongue down his throat, but decided against it.

When did you get out?" CoCo asked again.

"A couple of days ago."

"I can't believe this! Does that mean your lawyer was able to get the charges against you dismissed?"

"Yep!" he grinned, sweeping CoCo off her feet and lifting her up in the air.

"Baby, I'm so happy for you." When Genesis put her down, CoCo couldn't control herself. She reached her head up and placed her lips on his. But to her disappointment, Genesis gently pulled her away.

"CoCo, I asked Talisa to marry me."

"What?"

"She's pregnant. We're having a baby."

"Is that why you're marrying her?"

"No. You know how I feel about Talisa. She's the love of my life. But with going to jail and her carrying my child, I realize time is too precious to waste. I want her to be my wife."

CoCo turned away, devastated by the news. She didn't want Genesis to see the crushed look on her face or the tears that were surely decorating her eyes.

"Because I'm marrying Talisa doesn't mean I don't want you in my life."

"In your life how, Genesis?"

"Friends. We've always been such good friends. We bonded from day one."

"I don't know if I can deal with being around you like that. When I was locked up, I promised myself that if I ever saw you again I would tell you how much I love you. I've always loved you, Genesis."

"I love you too," he said, placing his hand on CoCo's cheek. "But I'm in love with Talisa."

"I see that now. I'm happy for you, but I'd be lying if I said that shit wasn't breaking my heart."

"That was never my intention."

"Talisa's a lucky woman."

"And I'm a lucky man to have her as my future wife, and you as my dear friend and hopefully business partner."

"Business partner?"

"If you're up for it. I gotta start stackin' paper again. I took a major 'L' with this whole federal case. I have a family to support now. I ain't got no choice but take advantage of this second chance I've been given. Plus, Quentin is willing to do whatever he can to get both of us back on our feet. I say we do it together. You down?"

"A few days ago I would've jumped at the

opportunity, but Chanel brought a proposition to me that I'm greatly considering."

"What sort of proposition?"

"I would no longer have to be directly involved in the drug trade, just give Arnez my connects and he would give me a percentage of all the profits."

"Yo' don't fuck with that nigga!"

"I know you and he don't like each other because of the whole Talisa situation, but this is business."

"It's more than that. That foul nigga is the reason Deuce is dead, and he will pay for that shit!"

"What the fuck are you talking about?"

"Yeah, he had put a hit out on me tryna eliminate the competition, but whoever he hired fucked up and killed the wrong person. Because Deuce and Antwon were getting something out of my car, the shooter assumed it was me."

"Are you serious?"

"Dead ass. That nigga is grimy. I'm telling you, don't trust him."

"I had no idea. I wonder if Chanel knows."

"I'm sure she does, which makes me wonder if she was involved in that shit in any way."

"Hell no! Chanel would never be a part of that! She knows how I feel about you. She would never co-sign on that bullshit with Arnez."

"If you say so, but definitely watch your back with that nigga. But you don't have to worry. Arnez ain't gonna be alive for much longer anyway."

"For the foul shit he's done, Arnez ain't got no place in my life anymore. I'm down for a partnership. Let's make this shit happen."

"That's what I'm talking about, baby girl!"

"Before I get all excited, you might be in the clear, but my shit's still lingering."

"Trust me, your lawyer will be calling you soon saying the prosecution is dropping the charges against you. Man, that judge told them my shit was dismissed with prejudice. You should've seen how those prosecutors' faces dropped. I'm still baffled how that shit went down."

"What did your lawyer say?"

"He was shocked too. He was shook for a minute."

"Why?"

"Because the supposed inside hookup he had to get the judge he wanted somehow fell through."

"What!"

"Yep. He thought it could go either way, but luckily it went our way. So, baby girl, trust me, you'll be good."

"I gotta feeling you might be right. So, in that case, where we setting up shop?"

"Philly, baby! Talisa and I are taking a flight out today. First, we're going to stop in New York. You know, it's time for me to meet the parents, especially since we're going to be family and all."

"From what I hear, Talisa has a pretty powerful

dad. How do you feel about that?"

"I have a great deal of respect for what he's accomplished. And as long as he understands I'm my own man and I follow my own rules, we're good."

"I'm sure it's going to all work out. And hopefully, I'll get the green light soon. When I do, I'll be joining you in Philly."

"I look forward to it."

Genesis gave CoCo a hug as he was about to leave, but she didn't want to let him go. Her heart wasn't ready to accept that they would never be, but her mind had to, so she walked him to the door and waved goodbye.

Chapter Twenty Two

We Need A Resolution

When Genesis drove up to the sprawling estate he was beyond impressed. The gated mansion nestled on top of the hill was the sort of lifestyle he envisioned providing for his family one day. Most young men would've been intimidated being with a woman whose father had reached such an abundance of success and wealth but not Genesis, he welcomed it. Having Jeffery Washington as a soon to be father-in-law, was the exact sort of motivation Genesis embraced.

"Baby, I'm so happy you're finally going to meet my parents."

"Me too. I have a lot to thank them for."

"Why do you say that?"

"If it wasn't for them, I wouldn't be marrying the woman of my dreams."

"Genesis, you say the sweetest things. I love you so much. You're going to be such a wonderful father." Talisa leaned over in her seat and gave Genesis a long kiss. They had been doing that every five minutes while in each other's company since Genesis was released from jail.

"Baby, before we go inside I want to show you something," Genesis said, reaching in his pocket for his wallet.

"What is it?"

"My mother walked out of my life when I was very young. I always hoped that one day she would come back and we would be a family again. It never happened, but I haven't given up hope. I wanted you to see this picture of her. I've never shared it with anybody."

For a moment Talisa was speechless. Then she looked up and stared at Genesis. "This woman looks like me."

"I know. That's why I was so drawn to you at first because you looked so much like my mother it was surreal. But that's where the similarities begin and end. You would never leave me the way that she did. You've proven that to me and now I'm finally able to let go of all the anger and pain I was holding on to."

"I had no idea you were keeping all of those

feelings bottled up inside. I'm glad you shared this with me."

"Me too."

"Whose baby is this?"

"My mothers'."

"You have a sister?"

"Yes, her name is Genevieve. But that was the first and last time I've ever seen her."

"You have a sister somewhere, you have to find her."

"I know. I've thought about that so many times. But right now I want to focus on taking care of you and our baby. After that, I'm going to do everything in my power to find her. With us getting married and having our baby, I truly understand the importance of family."

As Genesis got out of the car and walked to the door hand in hand with Talisa, he felt like for the first time, his life was perfect. All the stars were aligned in his favor and the path to greatness was his to take. Genesis raised Talisa's arm up and kissed her hand and said, "The world is ours, baby." All Talisa could do was smile in agreement.

"Daddy, how long have you all been standing there?" Talisa asked in surprise as her and Genesis reached the door.

"Long enough to see that my daughter is very much in love."

"And so am I sir, it's nice to finally meet you, I'm

Genesis Taylor." Genesis reached out and shook Mr. and Mrs. Washington's hand.

Mrs. Washington worked her eyes from the bottom to the top of Genesis' six-two, two hundred and ten pound solid muscle framed body. "Now I understand why my daughter is so smitten with you, you're stunning."

"Mother!" Talisa sighed in embarrassment.

"That's an interesting choice of words. I don't think I've ever been called stunning before." Genesis couldn't help but blush.

"You have to excuse my wife. She's never been one to hold back her thoughts."

"I guess that's where Talisa gets it from," he quipped.

"Be quiet," Talisa said, playfully hitting Genesis on his arm.

"Well now that we've been introduced, please come in." Genesis and Talisa followed her parents outside to the wrap-around covered terraces that lead to a heated mineral-water swimming pool. You could see the copper-and-slate-roofed pool house with a tiki bar, kitchen and large fireplace. The servants were already on alert, prepared to serve food and drinks at their request.

"I'm starving, and so is the baby so I'm going to get something to eat," Talisa said, rubbing her stomach. "Can I get you anything, baby?"

"No, I'm good, but thank," Genesis said, giving

Talisa a sweet kiss on the lips before she walked off.

"Genesis, do you mind if I have a word with you?"

"Of course not, what would you like to discuss with me, Mr. Washington."

"Call me Jeffery."

"Okay, Jeffery."

"I have to admit I was disappointed at first when I found out my daughter was pregnant and the father was in jail."

"That's understandable."

"I have no intentions of judging you and I understand as a man you have to make your own decisions. But so you know, it was because of me Judge Mantineo dismissed those charges against you."

"Excuse me, it was you?"

"Yes, I called in a huge favor. But I promised my daughter that I would do what I could to get you out of jail and home to her and the baby you all are about to bring into this world."

"Does Talisa know what you did?"

"No, and I have no intention of telling her. I'm telling you because I want you to know how much my daughters' happiness means to me. And I'm speaking as a father to you, who is about to become one. All I ask is that you protect my daughter and grandchild."

"First, I want to thank you for calling in that favor. Because of you, I'll be here to see my baby born. Second, I promise you, I will always protect Talisa and our child. They're everything to me."

"Thank you, that's all I wanted to hear. Also, if you ever decide you want to enter the corporate world. Do not hesitate to ask. I will make your transition as smooth as possible. We're family now and I'll do anything for my family."

"You're an incredible man, Mr. Washington…I mean Jeffery. And I'm proud to be a part of your family." The two men grasped hands and at that moment a lasting bond was formed.

*****

"Congratulations, CoCo! I just got off the phone with Robert Katz and he told me you're officially a free woman."

"Thanks Chanel. I have to admit it feels good to hear the words free and CoCo in the same sentence."

"I bet it does. So with your new free status, what are you going to do?"

"I'm actually about to catch a flight to Philly."

"Really? Are you coming to see me?"

"Of course I'ma see you while I'm there but my

first stop is to handle some business with Genesis."

"Have you put any thought into the business proposal I brought to you?"

"Yes. But after I found out what Arnez did, I don't ever want to fuck with him again."

"What are you talking about?"

"I hope that means you were not aware of the involvement he had in Deuce's death." Chanel swallowed hard, trying not to show any emotions.

"Of course not and I don't believe that he did. Why would Arnez want Deuce dead?"

"I'm not going to get into a long discussion with you about this over the phone, but Arnez did in fact have something to do with it. And just like I'm not fuckin' with him anymore, I would advise you to do the same."

"CoCo, I think you're making a mistake."

"The only mistake I made was using that nigga's money to ball out on. What he tried to do to Genesis but ended up doing to Deuce is foul and fucked up. I'm just relieved you weren't a part of it because then I would have to reassess my relationship with you too."

"What are you saying you would choose Genesis over me?"

"No, what I'm saying is that if you were in on such a pointless and vicious act, especially knowing how I feel about Genesis, I would have to question where your loyalty lies. Luckily that's not necessary because you didn't know but now you do…so cut that nigga Arnez off. I'll see you when I get to Philly." CoCo hung up the phone and it was evident the Boss Bitch was back.

Told You So

"Genesis, this warehouse is in a great location. We can do a lot of business but maintain privacy."

"Exactly, and that's how we're gonna have to move for a minute. You know the Feds got a hard-on for us now. They gon' be waiting for us to fuck up. But we have to learn from our prior mistakes—trust no one, and move in silence."

"Sure enough, we have to keep our eyes open, looking in the front, back, top, bottom and motherfuckin' sideways," CoCo joked, but was dead serious.

"Yeah, we 'bout to be overly cautious, which will save us in the end. We 'bout to go super hard, because within a year or two, we should've stacked enough paper to get out this game once and for all."

"I'm with you, partner."

"Did you tell your sister about our new partnership?"

"Sure did. She's actually on her way over here. I wanted her to see the spot too."

"How does she feel about us going into business together?"

"You know Chanel can be somewhat territorial, but she knows that in the big scheme of things, the three of us together can make major power moves."

"Indeed. Did you ever have a chance to speak to her about the Arnez shit?"

"Fuck yeah! Like I told you, she had no idea he had anything to do with that shit. But I told her now that she did know, to cut his trifling ass off for good."

"What did she say?"

"There was nothing to say. That shit wasn't debatable and Chanel understood that."

"Good. You told her right. Don't nobody need to be around that nigga, or they might end up becoming a casualty from being at the wrong place at the wrong time."

"We won't have that problem from Chanel. I set her straight."

*****

"I should've known it was only a matter of time before Talisa would tell Genesis I was responsible for Deuce's death. And of course, he couldn't wait to tell CoCo that shit." Arnez stood on his balcony, smoking a cigarette as the stress was now getting the best of him.

"What the fuck are we gonna do now? CoCo doesn't want anything to do with you, and she demanded I not fuck with you either. Nothing seems to be going according to plan."

"I know. With Genesis being out of jail and Delondo lurking around waiting for the right opportunity to take me down, shit is getting way too hot."

"So, what's our next move?"

"If there's no convincing CoCo, then it's lights out for her. Once she's dead, you can move in, that won't be a problem. But we need to do it fast before they start getting comfortable doing business with Genesis. If that happens, then again we'll be back in the same situation."

"I say we get rid of Genesis and CoCo at the same time."

"I understand your reasoning, but we have to be careful. We don't want fingers pointing back to us. Then we'll alienate a lot of the cats that were doing business with them, especially Quentin. I'm sure he knows my role in the Deuce situation, so he won't be fuckin' with me even after both of them are dead, but he will deal with you. Unless, of course, he finds out you had your hands all up in it too. You feel me?"

"Yes."

"So, we have to handle the situation with care. First, you take out CoCo, and then we work on getting Delondo, then Genesis."

"Genesis and CoCo are over at the warehouse now discussing business, and I'm supposed to stop by."

"That's cool. Do that. It's important you make everybody believe you're a team player."

"I'll handle CoCo. What's your next move?"

"I'ma get missing for a little while. That way when CoCo ends up dead, I won't be anywhere around. Then, while Genesis and Delondo are looking for me, I'll be somewhere plotting on them."

"I think that's smart. Do you have any idea where you're going?"

"I haven't decided yet, but once I get there, I'll make contact. You just be my eyes and ears here."

"Got you. Let me get to the warehouse. I don't need to raise anymore suspicions."

*****

When Chanel pulled up to the warehouse, the only car she saw was CoCo's. She was hoping that maybe Genesis rode with her sister and was still there. Chanel wanted to vibe him out to see if he believed her whole "I was in the dark act", or was there shade.

"CoCo, where are you?" Chanel yelled out when she entered the huge, darkly lit warehouse.

"I'm in the back! Here I come!" CoCo called out.

Chanel could hear the clicking of CoCo's heels as she made her way to the front. "Where's Genesis?" she asked when she saw her sister coming out alone.

"He just left about fifteen minutes ago. He's a busy boy. You know him and Talisa are getting married in the next few weeks."

"I didn't know. That must be hard on you."

"At first it was, but I'm starting to get used to the idea. I'm focusing on us making this money and that's it."

"You're doing the right thing, that's smart."

"So, how's everything with you?"

"Everything's good."

"So, you washed your hands of the whole Arnez situation?"

"Yep."

"When you confronted him, what did he say?"

"Not too much. At first he tried to deny it, but eventually he came clean."

"So, Arnez knows you're not fuckin' with him anymore?"

"Definitely."

CoCo wanted to believe her sister was being truthful with her, but she knew some shit didn't feel right. Instead of following her instants and delving deeper, her love for Chanel made her brush it off.

*****

Genesis wasn't in his crib for more than five minutes when his cell started going off. "What's up, Quentin?"

"You have a minute?"

"For you, I always got plenty," Genesis said, deciding to sit down and relax to make sure Quentin had his full attention. "Oh, and so you didn't think I forgot, after the wedding and the baby is born, if you need me to, I'll go back to Miami and find your daughter, Maya."

"Thank you. I would appreciate that. But first, take care of your family. You're about to be a new husband and father all in one month."

"And I am so looking forward to it. But enough about me. Back to the reason you called."

"A little while ago I was over at Martin's office."

"Martin, my attorney?"

"Yes."

"Oh fuck! The Feds aren't trying to fuck with me again, are they?"

"No, nothing like that."

"Then what?"

"He got a hold of some discovery papers that the prosecutors didn't originally turn over. I decided to go through them; you know, trying to see if I could make sense of a few things that weren't adding up to me. Like how Antwon got in that predicament in the first place, when only a handful of people knew about the trip. And more importantly, how one sister got busted, when it was supposedly a team operation. Then, I was stumped by how you got jammed up on that little detour adventure you took on my behalf. I recalled a conversation I had with a certain sister and mentioned Miami. You know, shit like that," Quentin alluded without trying to spell it all out, but he knew Genesis was following him.

"No doubt, I'm with you."

"I knew you would be." He paused before continuing. "So, it wasn't surprising that under a bunch of fluff talk and supposedly anonymous tips, buried in the paperwork, one of the informants was a C. Armstrong. We both know what that 'C' stands for."

"Yep! Motherfuckin' Chanel! I tried to tell CoCo her sister was knee-deep in this shit, but she wasn't tryna hear it."

"I think she'll listen to you now. But I can't blame CoCo. Nobody would want to believe that, not just your sister, but your twin, would sell you out. That's a hard pill for anybody to swallow."

"You're right, but the shit has to be dealt with. One thing I learned from Deuce's murder: never underestimate what your enemy is capable of doing. Chanel might be CoCo's sister, but she's also her enemy."

Chapter Twenty Four
The Jig Is Up

CoCo refused to believe that her twin sister, the person she loved more than anything in this world, would betray her. They were thicker than thieves, or so she thought. But as CoCo reflected back on incidents that didn't add up, she was forced to start realizing the truth — Chanel might not be the loyal sister whose allegiance to family came first and foremost.

The first incident that played out in CoCo's mind was the shooting at Arnez's birthday party. The shooters seemed to specifically target her. At first she thought that as always, Chanel was there to save the day, but maybe that wasn't the case. Maybe it was no coincidence, and the shit had been planned.

And then there was the murder of Chuck. CoCo remembered how Chanel was supposed to have met them that night at the party, and called to make sure they had arrived and wanted to know specifics as to where they would be in the club. But yet, she never showed up, and Chuck got killed protecting her. That was the incident that really made CoCo consider getting out the game once and for all.

Chuck had been like a surrogate father to her, especially after her dad died. Not only that, she considered him a friend and confidant. CoCo could discuss anything with Chuck, and never felt that he was judging her. She couldn't recall Chanel shedding one tear after his death. *I know Chanel didn't share the same closeness that I had with Chuck, but damn not one tear!* CoCo thought to herself as she entered the warehouse where she was meeting Chanel. Even with the doubts lurking in her head, she was still giving her sister the benefit of the doubt.

"Chanel, are you here?" CoCo called out, but didn't get an answer. There was no car out front, but she thought maybe Chanel had parked in the back. Right when she was about to call out her name again, her cell started ringing and she recognized the number. "Hey, you did say meet you at the warehouse, right?"

"Yeah, I'm running a little late. I'll be there in a few minutes.

"Cool. I'll be here." CoCo hung up the phone and sat down on a chair in the corner.

"In a few days, this place is going to be full of drugs," CoCo said out loud, scoping around the huge empty warehouse. After catching a break on their case, and the Feds dismissing the charges against her and Genesis, part of CoCo knew that they needed to give up "the life", but the money was calling their names. The Feds cleaned Genesis out money-wise, and CoCo wasn't much better off. Unless both wanted to struggle with a minimum wage job, this was it for them. Their only skill was that of hustling. And luckily, they had Quentin in their corner to get them back on their feet.

Ring...Ring...Ring

Who could this be? CoCo wondered before looking down at the number. "What's up?"

"Where are you?"

"At the warehouse."

"What you doing there?"

"About to meet Chanel."

"Yo', get the fuck up outta there!"

"Genesis, I know you have your suspicions, but I think you're wrong about Chanel."

"I'm not wrong. I have proof."

"What kind of proof?"

"I'll talk to you about it when you get here. Come to my crib, now!"

"Okay, I'm on my way."

Genesis could hear the reluctance in CoCo's voice. "Yo, I'm serious. Don't wait around there no longer. Come the fuck on!"

"A'ight. Here I come." CoCo hung up the phone and proceeded to leave.

"Where do you think you're going?" Chanel seemed to appear out of nowhere, and CoCo flinched, showing her surprise.

"I was just about to call you."

"No need now, I'm here."

"Quentin just called me, and I need to meet up with him right quick before he leaves to go back to LA. I'll call you when I'm done and we can hook back up."

"How about I ride with you?"

"There's no need. It shouldn't take that long."

"All the more reason I should come with you."

"That's okay. Plus, Quentin said he wanted to meet with me alone. You know how he is, and since he's my major supplier, I think it's best I follow his request."

"You mean *our*."

"Excuse me?"

"You used the word *my* when describing him as a supplier, when you should've said *our*. We are partners, remember."

"What type of question is that? Of course I remember."

"No need to get defensive."

"You're making me defensive."

Both sisters stood face-to-face as if ready for a showdown. Their demeanor wasn't representative of sisterly love, but more of sworn enemies.

"Chanel, if you have something to say, then say it. If not, move out the way because I need to meet Quentin and he doesn't like waiting."

"I do have something to say."

"Then hurry up and say it!" CoCo had been trying to remain calm and keep her temper in check, but Chanel's salty attitude was thrusting her closer to the edge.

"I want you to retire from the game and let Arnez have Quentin as his connect."

"What? Retire! I'm damn near broke and you're asking me to retire so the nigga you're fuckin' can swoop in take my shit? Are you smokin'?"

"You'll be financially compensated lovely."

"By who? Especially since you swore to me that your chips were low too. That, between paying my lawyer fees and supposedly being robbed and making some fucked up deals, our shit was practically on 'E' unless that was all a lie."

"It wasn't a lie. Arnez would be the one who would hit you off, to show his gratitude."

"Oh, so if I retire, are you going to retire too, or are you going to stand by your man and help him run his operation?"

"I haven't decided yet."

"Well, there's no need, because I ain't retiring from shit! Quentin is my connect, and he is going to get my money back right. Furthermore, I told you I wasn't fuckin' with Arnez no more after I found out he tried to have Genesis killed. Now excuse me, I have to go. I'm not wasting no more of my time discussing this bullshit!"

"You're not going anywhere," Chanel let it be known, stepping forward and invading the already small space between them.

CoCo stared deep into her sister's eyes, and at that very moment, it all became crystal clear. There were no more doubts or second guessing. Her sister was now only related to her by blood only. "You trifling bitch! It was you who set me up. It was your plan for me to spend the rest of my life rotting behind bars on those drug charges. But Antwon, the Fed's star witness getting killed, fucked that up for you and Arnez. The two of you thought you'd get rid of me and Genesis in one pop and have this whole drug shit on lock. You turned on your own sister for some dick! Our father must be turning in his grave right now."

"I tried to give you an opportunity to get out, but you wouldn't. You just couldn't let go. I was so tired of always being in your shadow, having to protect you. With Arnez, I would be right by his side, the head bitch in charge like it should have always been. Then, you forgot the rules of business and fell hard for Genesis, letting him deal directly with Quentin. I knew then it was time for you to bow out. You no longer knew how to keep your emotions in check. You were practically throwing him the pussy. The path you were on, you would've handed the keys to the empire we spent years building over to Genesis, and I would've been kicked to the curb."

"That's bullshit! Why don't you admit you sold me out for some dick so we can move on. Now excuse me, I have to go." CoCo moved to the side to step around her sister, but Chanel latched onto her arm, gripping it tightly. In the mist of their tugging, CoCo heard her cell ringing, and when she yanked her arm away to answer, Chanel grabbed it from her hand and threw it across the room.

CoCo then lunged for her sister's throat, but Chanel lifted up her stiletto boot and kicked her in the stomach, sending CoCo flying backwards and falling to the floor.

"I thought you knew you couldn't beat me. You never could, and that shit ain't changed," Chanel gloated.

CoCo jumped to her feet, not willing to be

defeated. She did know her sister was more so of the fighter between the two, not because she couldn't hold her own, but that was the role Chanel had played and CoCo never had the need to challenge it... until now.

"I am gonna whoop your ass, and I'm gonna take great pleasure in doing so," CoCo promised, popping her knuckles, preparing for an all-out brawl.

"As much as I would like to indulge you, I don't have time. Arnez is waiting for me. And I know Quentin is waiting for you too, but unfortunately, you won't be showing up," Chanel divulged, taking out her 9mm semi automatic with a silencer, pointing it directly at her sister.

"You're planning on killing me?"

"Don't look so surprised. You know I was born a killer."

"Chanel, we're sisters...twins! What the fuck is going on in your head? It's one thing to have me locked up, but murder is something else. You don't want my blood on your hands."

"Don't beg. Take this bullet like the soldier you were taught to be."

"We're better than this! I don't give a fuck what you say, ain't no way you're taking me out. We've been through too much shit together. We're like this," CoCo crossed her index and middle fingers, hoping she could get through to her sister. She loathed Chanel for what she had done, but CoCo loved her even more and believed she could reach her.

"Drop your gun!" Genesis yelled out, sneaking up on them.

CoCo and Chanel turned simultaneously in his direction, surprised by his entrance.

"Genesis, thank God you're here! Chanel was about to kill me! Luckily I was able to pull out my gun before she got to hers."

"Genesis, she's lying! I'm CoCo, she's Chanel!" the real CoCo said, pointing at her sister.

But Genesis was stumped. They truly looked identical, especially since both were now sporting the same short haircut. He was completely unsure which one was which.

"Genesis, don't listen to her. I confronted her about Arnez, Chuck…"

"I knew you had something to do with Chuck's death," CoCo blurted out, cutting Chanel off.

"Of course you knew, Chanel, since you were the one who set it up. Then working with Arnez to have Genesis' killed, but instead, his best friend ended up dead. Now you're trying to kill me. You're definitely not the sister I thought you were."

Genesis looked at both women trying to find one mark to distinguish them apart, but he kept coming up empty. "Put the gun down!"

"But Genesis, it's me, CoCo!"

"Just put the gun down until I figure this shit out."

Chanel obliged his request and placed the gun down on the floor.

"Neither one of you move." He started from the bottom and worked his way to the top, but they were identical in not only looks, but in style. Then he started thinking of a question he could ask that only the real CoCo would know the answer to.

"Genesis, listen to me. You were right when you said Chanel was behind this bullshit. I didn't want to believe you, but you were right. So please, don't let her trick you like she has been tricking me," Chanel pleaded. Her performance sounded so bona fide that if CoCo wasn't the real deal, she would've been convinced. And obviously, so was Genesis, because he pointed his gun at his target, and unbeknownst to him, it was the wrong sister.

"Go ahead, kill her, Genesis, so she can never hurt us again," Chanel said, pressing him on as she tried to reach for her other gun on the sly.

"You have to be Chanel, because the real CoCo would never wish death on her sister."

As Genesis was redirecting his weapon from pointing in CoCo's direction, Chanel was able to use the slight distraction he had to reach for her hidden gun. Genesis caught the flash of the steel as Chanel lifted up her firearm with her finger steady on the trigger, ready to shoot. Not giving her the chance to execute and without a second thought, Genesis blasted two shots into Chanel's torso. As the blood gushed out, she put her hand over the open gash as in disbelief that she had been shot. It wasn't until she saw the blood seeping through her fingers that she realized the bullets had ripped her chest wide open.

"Oh God...Chanel!" CoCo cried out, reaching for her sister who had bent down to her knees before falling flat down on her back.

"I've been shot," Chanel mumbled in shock as blood leaked from her mouth.

"Shhh! Don't say another word. You're gonna be okay, just relax," CoCo begged, as she cradled her sister in her arms. But both of them knew that wasn't true. Chanel was dying in her arms and there was nothing either one of them could do to stop it.

Chanel squeezed her sister's hand tightly and whispered, "Forgive me."

"I do...please don't die, Chanel...please don't!" Chanel's body jerked and she released her sister's hand. "Now I *do* have the blood of my sister on my hands." CoCo closed her eyes as the tears rained down.

Chapter Twenty Five

Genevieve

Talisa placed her hand on her protruding belly and rubbed it gently. "Today, I will be Mrs. Genesis Taylor," she beamed in the full-length mirror, admiring her silhouette in the flowing white, empire waist wedding dress. It had a soft, elegant, extremely feminine goddess-like appearance that made her natural pregnancy glow come alive even more.

After all the obstacles Talisa and Genesis had to endure, it was worth it for her to walk down the aisle so they could become man and wife. The small intimate wedding was the perfect touch to such a sacred and monumental moment in their lives. With the baby due in a couple of weeks, they pulled out all the stops to make sure they were officially united as one before their child was born.

Talisa did a final twirl in front of the mirror, then grabbed her bouquet of flowers to begin the new life that was awaiting her.

The outdoor wedding at Bartram's Garden in Philadelphia was the perfect combination for a city and country wedding. The elegant 18th century riverfront estate set on 45 acres of preserved gardens, and the country's oldest botanical garden, had the sort of long withstanding beauty and purity they prayed their marriage would reflect.

"Are you ready?" Talisa's father asked, as they were about to make their way to the garden.

An enthused nervousness sparked inside of Talisa as she stared out at the wetlands, rolling lawns and the Philadelphia skyline that all seemed to be welcoming her.

"Yes, Daddy, I'm ready." Talisa interlocked her arm with her father's, and they began to make her way to the man she would spend the rest of her life with.

The late afternoon breeze brushed against CoCo's face as she sat next to Quentin, waiting for the ceremony to begin. She glanced over at Genesis, who was the picture of perfection in his Armani tuxedo. Although the love she felt for Genesis had never strayed, CoCo knew he was deeply in love with Talisa, which made her genuinely happy that the two of them would be exchanging vows to become husband and wife.

On a day that was about love and new beginnings, CoCo kept reflecting on the past and lost love – her sister Chanel. It had been over a month since she died, but it seemed like yesterday. CoCo hadn't come to grips with how it all went so wrong. She had wanted to confront Arnez about turning her sister against her, because she needed someone to blame, and he seemed like the perfect candidate. After word quickly spread about Chanel's death, Arnez vanished and no one knew his whereabouts. But both Genesis and CoCo were determined to get their revenge on him. They didn't care how long it would take.

As CoCo harped on seeking revenge on Arnez, her thoughts were interrupted as Talisa's mother stood up, signaling the guests to do the same as the bride walked down the aisle. CoCo had to admit to herself that Talisa looked absolutely stunning. She was truly glowing, and CoCo didn't know if it was due to her pregnancy, or because she was marrying the man she loved. She decided it was a combination of both.

"They make a beautiful couple," Quentin

commented to CoCo.

"They certainly do." CoCo watched as the two pledged their undying love, devotion and support to each other, and as much as it broke her heart, she knew that she had to let go. Genesis would never be hers. He was marrying the woman he loved, about to bring a child into this world, and they would be a family. Accepting that almost brought tears to CoCo's eyes, but she was a soldier and would no doubt march on.

"I want to thank everyone for being here. As you can see, we have a very small but important group of people in attendance. Unfortunately, one of the most significant people to me, Deuce, may he rest in peace, couldn't be here to celebrate the happiest day of my life. But I've been blessed with so much," he continued, gazing lovingly into Talisa's eyes. "I've married my soul mate, and very soon we will be welcoming into this world what our love has produced," Genesis smiled.

"I love you, baby," Talisa said, through tears.

"I love you too. And on that note, our Maybach awaits us. It's honeymoon time!" Genesis literally swept Talisa off her feet and carried her to the waiting car. The handful of guests trailed behind them, cheering for the lovebirds. The image of the two of them seemed to be something straight out of a magazine. No one had ever seen Genesis look so happy and even playful like a little boy as he twirled Talisa around before getting in the car.

But some dreams aren't meant to be fulfilled into reality, and the ringing of the machine gun signified that. What a few seconds ago was the epitome of a picturesque scene was now a bloodbath. Love, hope and peace deserted the air, and death took its place.

*****

"He gets more beautiful everyday, Genesis. I can't believe he's six months old already," CoCo said, holding Amir in her arms.

Genesis stood up from the couch and walked outside to the balcony. As much as he adored his son, each day, week and month that passed was a reminder that although he gained a son, he lost his wife and the mother of his child.

Watching her die remained vivid in his mind. The happiest day of this life turned out to be the worst. One minute they were both smiling as he twirled her around, and the next, the pure white of Talisa's dress had turned blood red. On the way to the hospital, he knew she was barely holding on, but in his mind there was no way he was so cursed that in his short life he could lose both his best friend and his new bride—but he did. The doctors did everything they could to save Talisa, but her injuries were too severe. It was a miracle his son survived, and for that he would be eternally grateful.

"I didn't want to bother you, but your phone keeps ringing and I thought it might be important," CoCo said, handing Genesis his cell.

"Thanks." He looked down at the number and it was marked private. At first he wasn't going to answer, but something made him. "Hello," he said, with hesitation.

"Is this Genesis?"

"Who wants to know?"

"Your sister…Genevieve."

Want the full story behind Genesis' sister Genevieve…read **Trife Life To Lavish Series**

Chapter 1
Underground King

Alex stepped into his attorney's office to discuss what was always his number one priority...business. When he sat down their eyes locked and there was complete silence for the first few seconds. This was Alex's way of setting the tone of the meeting. His silence spoke volumes. This might've been his attorney's office but he was the head nigga in charge and nothing got started until he decided it was time to speak. Alex felt this approach was necessary. You see, after all these years of them doing business, attorney George Lofton still wasn't used to dealing with a man like Alex; a dirt-poor kid who could've easily died in the projects he was born in, but instead had made millions. It wasn't done the ski mask way but it was still illegal.

They'd first met when Alex was a sixteen-year-old kid growing up in TechWood Homes, a housing project in Atlanta. Alex and his best friend, Deion, had been arrested because the principal found 32 crack vials in Alex's book bag. Another kid had tipped the principal off and the principal subsequently called the police. Alex and Deion were arrested and suspended from school. His mother called George, who had the charges against them dismissed, and they were allowed to go back to school. But that wasn't the last time he would use George. He was arrested at twenty-two for attempted murder, and for trafficking cocaine a year later. Alex was acquitted on both charges. George Lofton later became known as the best trial attorney in Atlanta, but Alex had also become the best at what he did. And since it was Alex's money that kept Mr. Lofton in designer suits, million dollar homes and foreign cars, he believed he called the shots, and dared his attorney to tell him otherwise.

Alex noticed that what seemed like a long period of silence made Mr. Lofton feel uncomfortable, which he liked. Out of habit, in order to camouflage the discomfort, his attorney always kept bottled water within arm's reach. He would cough, take a swig, and lean back in his chair, raising his eyebrows a little, trying to give a look of certainty, though he wasn't completely confident at all in Alex's presence. The reason was because Alex did what many had thought would be impossible, especially men like George Lofton. He had gone from a knucklehead, low-level drug dealer to an underground king and an unstoppable respected criminal boss.

Before finally speaking, Alex gave an intense stare into George Lofton's piercing eyes. They were not only the bluest he had ever seen, but also some of the most calculating. The latter is what Alex found so compelling. A calculating attorney working on his behalf could almost guarantee a get out of jail free card for the duration of his criminal career.

"Have you thought over what we briefly discussed the other day?" Alex asked his attorney, finally breaking the silence.

"Yes I have, but I want to make sure I understand you correctly. You want to give me six hundred thousand to represent you or your friend Deion if you are ever arrested and have to stand trial again in the future?"

Alex assumed he had already made himself clear based on their previous conversations and was annoyed by what he now considered a repetitive question. "George, you know I don't like repeating myself. That's exactly what I'm saying. Are we clear?"

"So this is an unofficial retainer."

"Yes, you can call it that."

George stood and closed the blinds then walked over to the door that led to the reception area. He turned the deadbolt so they wouldn't be disturbed. George sat back behind the desk. "You know that if you and your friend Deion are ever on the same case that I can't represent the both of you."

"I know that."

"So what do you propose I do if that was ever to happen?"

"You would get him the next best attorney in Atlanta," Alex said without hesitation. Deion was Alex's best friend—had been since the first grade. They were now business partners, but the core of their bond was built on that friendship, and because of that Alex would always look out for Deion's best interest.

"That's all I need to know."

Alex clasped his hands and stared at the ceiling for a moment, thinking that maybe it was a bad idea bringing the money to George. Maybe he should have just put it somewhere safe only known to him and his mom. He quickly dismissed his concerns.

"Okay. Where's the money?" Alex presented George with two leather briefcases. He opened the first one and was glad to see that it was all hundred-dollar bills. When he closed the briefcase he asked, "There is no need to count this is there?"

"You can count it if you want, but it's all there."

George took another swig of water. The cash made him nervous. He planned to take it directly to one of his bank safe deposit boxes. The two men stood. Alex was a foot taller than George; he had flawless mahogany skin, a deep brown with a bit of a red tint, broad shoulders, very large hands, and a goatee. He was a man's man. With such a powerful physical appearance, Alex kept his style very low-key. His only display of wealth was a pricey diamond watch that his best friend and partner Deion had bought him for his birthday.

"I'll take good care of this, and you," his attorney said, extending his hand to Alex.

"With this type of money, I know you will," Alex stated without flinching. Alex gave one last lingering stare into his attorney's piercing eyes. "We do have a clear understanding…correct?"

"Of course. I've never let you down and I never will. That, I promise you." The men shook hands and

Alex made his exit with the same coolness as his entrance.

With Alex embarking on a new, potentially dangerous business venture, he wanted to make sure that he had all his bases covered. The higher up he seemed to go on the totem pole, the costlier his problems became. But Alex welcomed new challenges because he had no intention of ever being a nickel and dime nigga again.

Read The Entire Bitch Series in This Order

P.O. Box 912
Collierville, TN 38027

A KING PRODUCTION

www.joydejaking.com
www.twitter.com/joydejaking

ORDER FORM

Name:

Address:

City/State:

Zip:

QUANTITY	TITLES	PRICE	TOTAL
	Bitch	$15.00	
	Bitch Reloaded	$15.00	
	The Bitch Is Back	$15.00	
	Queen Bitch	$15.00	
	Last Bitch Standing	$15.00	
	Superstar	$15.00	
	Ride Wit' Me	$12.00	
	Ride Wit' Me Part 2	$15.00	
	Stackin' Paper	$15.00	
	Trife Life To Lavish	$15.00	
	Trife Life To Lavish II	$15.00	
	Stackin' Paper II	$15.00	
	Rich or Famous	$15.00	
	Rich or Famous Part 2	$15.00	
	Rich or Famous Part 3	$15.00	
	Bitch A New Beginning	$15.00	
	Mafia Princess Part 1	$15.00	
	Mafia Princess Part 2	$15.00	
	Mafia Princess Part 3	$15.00	
	Mafia Princess Part 4	$15.00	
	Mafia Princess Part 5	$15.00	
	Boss Bitch	$15.00	
	Baller Bitches Vol. 1	$15.00	
	Baller Bitches Vol. 2	$15.00	
	Baller Bitches Vol. 3	$15.00	
	Bad Bitch	$15.00	
	Still The Baddest Bitch	$15.00	
	Power	$15.00	
	Power Part 2	$15.00	
	Drake	$15.00	
	Drake Part 2	$15.00	
	Female Hustler	$15.00	
	Female Hustler Part 2	$15.00	
	Female Hustler Part 3	$15.00	
	Female Hustler Part 4	$15.00	
	Female Hustler Part 5	$15.00	
	Female Hustler Part 6	$15.00	
	Princess Fever "Birthday Bash"	$6.00	
	Nico Carter The Men Of The Bitch Series	$15.00	
	Bitch The Beginning Of The End	$15.00	
	Supreme...Men Of The Bitch Series	$15.00	
	Bitch The Final Chapter	$15.00	
	Stackin' Paper III	$15.00	
	Men Of The Bitch Series And The Women Who Love Them	$15.00	
	Coke Like The 80s	$15.00	
	Baller Bitches The Reunion Vol. 4	$15.00	
	Stackin' Paper IV	$15.00	
	The Legacy	$15.00	
	Lovin' Thy Enemy	$15.00	
	Stackin' Paper V	$15.00	
	The Legacy Part 2	$15.00	
	Assassins - Episode 1	$11.00	
	Assassins - Episode 2	$11.00	
	Assassins - Episode 2	$11.00	
	Bitch Chronicles	$40.00	
	So Hood So Rich	$15.00	
	Stackin' Paper VI	$15.00	
	Female Hustler Part 7	$15.00	
	Toxic...	$6.00	

Shipping/Handling (Via Priority Mail) $8.95 1-3 Books, $16.25 4-7 Books. For 7 or more $21.50.
Total: $_____ FORMS OF ACCEPTED PAYMENTS: Certified or government issued checks and money Orders, all mail in orders take 5-7 Business days to be delivered

www.ingramcontent.com/pod-product-compliance
Lightning Source LLC
Chambersburg PA
CBHW030149100526
44592CB00009B/189